IBEW APTITUDE TEST PREP 2025

The Complete Study Guide for Passing the IBEW Aptitude Test

Table of Contents

Introduction: IBEW Aptitude Test Essentials..9

The IBEW in Brief..9

   Union Support for Electricians..9

The Apprenticeship Program..10

   How It Works: Paid Training..10

   Entry Requirements...10

About the Aptitude Test..11

   Math and Reading Skills Assessment..11

   Test Format: Algebra & Reading Comprehension....................12

Test Structure & Scoring...13

   Timing and Questions...13

   Passing Score...14

   When You'll Get Results...15

Chapter 1: Number Properties and Operations.........................17

1.1: Types and Behavior of Numbers..17

   Types of Numbers...17

   Even, Odd, and Prime Numbers...18

   Divisibility Rules...19

1.2: Core Mathematical Laws...20

   Commutative, Associative, Distributive Laws...........................20

   Identity and Inverse Properties...21

Chapter 2: Basic Arithmetic Skills..23

2.1: Efficient Calculation Techniques...23

   Addition & Subtraction Shortcuts..23

   Multiplication & Division Strategies...24

2.2: Estimation and Mixed Practice..25

   Estimation and Rounding..25

   Mixed Operations...26

Chapter 3: Fractions and Decimals..28

3.1: Understanding and Converting...28

   Fraction Basics...28

   Fraction-Decimal Conversion...29

3.2: Fraction and Decimal Operations..30

   Add, Subtract, Multiply, Divide Fractions................................30

   Decimal Operations..31

   Key Concepts for Decimal Operations:.....................................32

Chapter 4: Exponents and Roots 34

4.1 : Mastering Exponents...34

Basics and Notation 34

Exponent Rules Simplification 35

4.2 : Roots and Their Uses 36

Square and Cube Numbers 36

Roots and Simplification...37

Chapter 5: Order of Operations (PEMDAS)..38

5.1 : Applying the PEMDAS Rule...38

PEMDAS Sequence 38

Complex Expressions 39

5.2 : Practice and Pitfalls 40

Avoiding Mistakes 40

Timed Drills for Speed and Confidence 40

Chapter 6: Percents, Ratios & Proportions 42

6.1 : Percent Concepts and Calculations 42

Understanding Percents 42

Conversions: Percent, Decimal, Fraction 43

6.2 : Ratios and Proportions..44

Ratios and Rates..44

Solving Proportions with Cross-Multiplication 45

Word Problems: Percent and Ratio Skills..46

Chapter 7: Word Problem Strategies 48

7.1 : Solving Word Problems Effectively..48

Translating to Math...48

Spotting Clues 49

Common Word Problem Types...50

Practice Sets and Solutions 51

Chapter 8: Algebra Basics 53

8.1 : Core Concepts 53

What Is Algebra? 53

Expressions vs. Equations 54

Using Variables in Context 55

8.2 : Language and Structure...56

Algebra Vocabulary 56

Order of Operations in Algebra...57

Chapter 9: Linear Equations 58

9.1 : Simplifying and Solving...58

Simplifying Expressions...58

Solving Equations Step-by-Step...59

9.2 : Application and Strategy..60

    Word Problems Solving with Equations...60

    Common Mistakes in Solving Equations...61

Chapter 10: Systems of Equations...62

10.1 : Solving Techniques...62

    What Are Systems? Solving Two Variables 62

    Substitution & Elimination Methods..63

10.2 : Visual & Real-World Applications...65

    Graphical Solutions...65

    Application Problems..66

Chapter 11: Quadratic Equations..69

11.1 : Solving Quadratics...69

    Recognizing Quadratics..69

    Factoring & Quadratic Formula...70

    Completing the Square..71

11.2 : Graphing Quadratics..71

    Parabolas: Graphs and Analysis..71

Chapter 12: Polynomials & Factoring...73

12.1 : Working with Polynomials...73

    Understanding Polynomials...73

    Adding & Subtracting: Combine Like Terms...74

12.2 : Multiplication and Factoring...75

    Multiplying Polynomials with FOIL Method..75

    Factoring Trinomials and Special Identities..76

Chapter 13: Rational Expressions..77

13.1 : Core Operations...77

    Rational Expressions Defined..77

    Simplifying: Factor and Reduce...78

13.2 : Arithmetic and Solving...79

    Multiplying & Dividing: Cross-Cancellation..79

    Adding & Subtracting Expressions...80

    Solving Equations: Isolate the Variable..82

Chapter 14: Inequalities & Absolute Value..84

14.1 : Inequalities...84

    Solving Linear Inequalities..84

    Graphing Solutions on Number Lines..85

    Compound Inequalities: And/Or Cases..86

14.2 : Absolute Value..87

Absolute Value as Distance from Zero 87

Solving Equations & Inequalities 88

Chapter 15: Functions & Graphs 90

15.1 : Function Basics 90

What Is a Function? 90

Function Notation and Evaluation 91

15.2 : Types and Graphing...92

Linear vs Nonlinear Patterns 92

Graphing with Slope and Intercepts.. 93

Real-World Models 94

Chapter 16: Function Information Analysis 96

16.1 : Graph Interpretation 96

Domain & Range 96

Key Graph Features... 97

Increasing/Decreasing Intervals 97

16.2 : Representation & Translation...98

Tables & Graphs 98

Translating Forms 99

Chapter 17: Number & Pattern Series 101

17.1 : Recognizing Sequences 101

Arithmetic Sequences 101

17.2 : Rules and Challenges 102

Finding the Next Term.. 102

Writing Rules for Algebraic Sequences 103

Visual Patterns 105

Chapter 18: Probability & Statistics 106

18.1 : Core Concepts 106

Probability Basics... 106

Theoretical vs Experimental Data 107

18.2 : Working with Data 108

Mean, Median, Mode, Range 108

Charts & Graphs Interpretation... 109

Word Problems in Stats and Probability 110

Chapter 19: Geometry Essentials 112

19.1 : Shapes and Properties 112

Lines and Angles 112

Perimeter & Area Formulas for 2D Shapes.. 113

19.2 : 3D and Coordinate Geometry 115

Volume & Surface Area of Solids.. 115

Pythagorean Theorem Applications 116

Coordinate Geometry Basics 117

Chapter 20: Applied Trigonometry 119

20.1 : Trigonometric Basics 119

SOHCAHTOA Basics 119

Solving Triangles with Trigonometry 120

20.2 : Real-World Applications 121

Word Problems: Trig in Height & Distance 121

Angles of Elevation and Depression 122

Calculator Shortcuts 123

Chapter 21: Reading Comprehension Skills 125

21.1 : Understanding the Test & Active Reading 125

Reading Comprehension Basics 125

Types of Texts on the Test 126

Active Reading Techniques 127

21.2 : Identifying Main Ideas and Purpose 128

Finding the Main Idea 128

Author's Purpose and Tone 129

Topic Sentences and Traps 130

21.3 : Details, Evidence, and Organization 131

Supporting Details 131

Logical Flow of Ideas 132

Eliminating Wrong Answers 133

21.4 : Making Inferences 134

Inference Skills 134

Types of Inference Questions 135

Avoid Overthinking 136

21.5 : Contextual Vocabulary 137

Using Context Clues 137

Eliminating Incorrect Word Choices 138

Technical Vocabulary in Context 139

21.6 : Technical and Workplace Texts 140

Reading Instructions and Manuals 140

Cause and Effect in Procedures 141

Drawing Conclusions from Data 142

Acknowledgements 144

SCAN THE QR CODE AT THE END OF THE BOOK TO ACCESS THE BONUSES

Introduction: IBEW Aptitude Test Essentials

The IBEW in Brief

Union Support for Electricians

The International Brotherhood of Electrical Workers (IBEW) plays an essential role in providing comprehensive support to electricians and apprentices by establishing a meticulously structured framework that encompasses extensive training, rigorous education, and strategic facilitation of job access. This union creates an environment where the dissemination of specialized knowledge, adherence to stringent safety standards, and enhancement of technical proficiency are of utmost importance.

The training programs orchestrated by the IBEW are characterized by a dual-faceted approach that integrates in-depth theoretical instruction with extensive practical application. Apprentices are immersed in an experiential learning process where they acquire practical skills through direct, hands-on involvement under the supervision of highly experienced professionals. This practical training is seamlessly integrated with classroom-based instruction, where apprentices explore the intricacies of contemporary electrical theory, gain a comprehensive understanding of current code standards, and internalize the latest safety practices. This methodical approach ensures that apprentices not only develop a robust set of technical skills but also attain a profound understanding of the theoretical principles that underpin their practical work.

Facilitating access to employment opportunities is a critical component of the IBEW's mission. The union employs a strategic approach to secure job placements for its members by leveraging its expansive network within the electrical industry to create connections between electricians and prospective employers. Through the process of collective bargaining, the IBEW advocates vigorously for equitable wages, comprehensive benefits, and optimal working conditions, thereby safeguarding the rights and promoting the welfare of its members within the workplace.

Prospective members of the IBEW encounter the aptitude test as a pivotal hurdle in their journey. This examination is carefully designed to assess candidates' proficiency in mathematical reasoning and reading comprehension, skills regarded as essential for success in the apprenticeship program and advancement in the electrical trade. Thorough preparation for this test is crucial, as it not only determines eligibility for entry into the apprenticeship program but also establishes a foundational basis for a successful and enduring career in the electrical industry.

The Apprenticeship Program

How It Works: Paid Training

The IBEW Apprenticeship Program meticulously integrates structured classroom instruction with practical, on-the-job training to equip apprentices with the comprehensive skills necessary for a successful career in the electrical industry. This dual-faceted approach ensures that participants not only master advanced electrical theories and adhere to the most current code standards but also effectively translate this theoretical knowledge into practical applications within real-world environments.

Classroom instruction forms the foundational layer of the program, emphasizing a detailed exploration of electrical theory, intricate code standards, stringent safety protocols, and other critical areas of knowledge. The curriculum is delivered by seasoned professionals with extensive industry experience through a combination of in-depth lectures, live demonstrations of complex electrical phenomena, and interactive discussions that encourage critical thinking and problem-solving. This setup allows apprentices to delve into the intricacies of electrical concepts, pose insightful questions, and actively engage with the material. Rigorous assessments, designed to challenge their comprehension, are employed to evaluate their understanding of the material and readiness for practical implementation.

The hands-on training component is carefully designed to complement and enhance the theoretical learning by immersing apprentices in authentic work environments under the guidance of experienced journeyman electricians. Apprentices are tasked with executing a variety of electrical operations, such as detailed wiring configurations, precise installation procedures, and systematic troubleshooting across diverse project settings, including residential, commercial, and industrial sites. This experiential learning phase is critical for apprentices to refine their technical skills, acclimate to the physical demands of the trade, and acquire a nuanced understanding of the complexities inherent in electrical work.

The program employs a meticulously structured approach to synchronizing classroom education with practical training, ensuring that apprentices progress at a pace that aligns with their individual skill acquisition and development. Continuous evaluations and structured feedback sessions are integral to the program, serving to identify areas of proficiency and those requiring enhancement. This targeted feedback facilitates a personalized learning trajectory that addresses the unique needs and learning pace of each apprentice, thereby optimizing their professional growth and competence in the field.

Entry Requirements

To qualify for the IBEW Apprenticeship Program, candidates must satisfy a set of stringent entry requirements designed to evaluate their preparedness and potential to thrive in the electrical trade. These criteria are meticulously crafted to ensure that each apprentice possesses the essential foundational skills required for the demanding training regimen and the professional challenges they will encounter.

Applicants are required to possess a high school diploma or GED, underscoring the necessity of a fundamental comprehension of mathematics, science, and English. Mastery of these subjects is critical for understanding technical manuals, electrical codes, and safety regulations, which are integral to the trade. A robust understanding of algebra is imperative, as the aptitude test prominently features algebraic reasoning components. Candidates must demonstrate proficiency in manipulating variables, solving linear equations, and understanding functions, such as $y = mx + b$ which are pivotal for addressing the mathematical complexities inherent in electrical work.

Prospective apprentices must be at least 18 years old. This requirement aligns with legal standards for employment within the electrical industry, ensuring that applicants have attained a level of maturity and personal responsibility that is conducive to both the learning environment and workplace dynamics.

Physical fitness is a non-negotiable aspect of the qualification process, given the physically demanding nature of electrical work. Candidates are expected to perform tasks that necessitate manual dexterity, such as handling small components and tools, as well as tasks requiring significant strength, such as lifting heavy equipment. Additionally, climbing ladders and working in diverse environmental conditions, including confined spaces or at heights, are common. Although specific fitness benchmarks are not explicitly stated, the ability to safely and efficiently conduct physical labor is essential.

Possessing a valid driver's license and access to reliable transportation is often a prerequisite, reflecting the practical need for apprentices to commute to various job sites, educational classes, or workshops. These locations may not be conveniently accessible via public transportation, necessitating personal mobility.

Successfully passing the IBEW aptitude test is a pivotal component of the application process. Achieving a score that meets or surpasses the threshold set by the local union is indicative of the candidate's competency in mathematics and reading comprehension, both of which are foundational to the structured apprenticeship curriculum.

About the Aptitude Test

Math and Reading Skills Assessment

The IBEW Aptitude Test is designed to rigorously assess the specific mathematical and reading comprehension skills that are fundamentally required for proficiency and success in the electrical trade. A thorough understanding of the test's objectives enables candidates to strategically direct their preparation efforts toward the most pertinent and impactful areas.

The Math Skills Assessment is heavily focused on algebraic concepts and functional analysis, both of which are indispensable in the electrical sector. Candidates must achieve a high level of competence in solving linear equations and understanding linear functions, typically expressed in the form $y = mx + b$, where m denotes the slope, representing the rate of change, and indicates the y-intercept, which is the point at which the line crosses the y-axis. This understanding is crucial for accurately determining electrical current flow and calculating voltage drop across various circuit configurations. Additionally, candidates must demonstrate adeptness in fundamental arithmetic operations, including addition, subtraction, multiplication, and division, as well as proficient handling of fractions and decimals. Mastery of quadratic equations, represented by the standard form $ax^2 + bx + c = 0$, is also essential, requiring candidates to identify real or complex roots using methods such as factoring, completing the square, or applying the quadratic formula. Practical strategies for success include gaining fluency with the distributive property, expressed as $a(b + c) = ab + ac$, which is vital for simplifying complex algebraic expressions. Moreover, candidates should develop the ability to adeptly manipulate and solve for variables within algebraic equations, ensuring precision and accuracy in their calculations.

The Reading Comprehension section evaluates the candidate's capacity to thoroughly understand and interpret technical materials, which may include electrical manuals, safety regulations, and detailed installation instructions. Effective preparation involves the implementation of active reading strategies that enhance retention and comprehension of intricate texts. Candidates should focus on identifying the main idea, discerning supporting details, and understanding the author's intent. The ability to make logical inferences based on textual evidence and to comprehend technical vocabulary within its specific context is of paramount importance. To build these skills, candidates should engage with a diverse array of technical documents, actively practice summarizing the content, and work on improving both comprehension speed and accuracy.

Candidates are advised to integrate these mathematical and reading comprehension skills into their daily study routines, utilizing practice tests as a means to measure progress and identify areas that require further development. Emphasizing the application of problem-solving techniques under timed conditions can effectively simulate the actual test environment, thereby enhancing both confidence and efficiency in tackling the assessment.

Test Format: Algebra & Reading Comprehension

The IBEW Aptitude Test is composed of two primary components: the Algebra & Functions section and the Reading Comprehension section. These components are meticulously designed to evaluate the core competencies required for a successful career in the electrical industry. A thorough comprehension of the intricacies within each section enables candidates to strategize their preparation with precision and efficiency.

In the Algebra & Functions section, candidates are presented with a series of problems that rigorously assess their proficiency in manipulating and solving various algebraic expressions and equations. This section demands a comprehensive understanding of linear equations, which involves analyzing the interplay between variables through equations structured in the format $y = mx + b$. Here, m denotes the slope, representing the rate of change between the dependent variable y and the independent variable x, while b indicates the y-intercept, the point at which the line intersects the y-axis. Mastery of these concepts is essential for interpreting complex electrical diagrams and accurately calculating parameters such as current, voltage, and resistance within electrical circuits. Furthermore, candidates are evaluated on their ability to solve quadratic equations, expressed in the standard form $ax^2 + bx + c = 0$. This requires adeptness in employing techniques such as factoring, which involves breaking down the equation into simpler binomial expressions, completing the square to transform the equation into a perfect square trinomial, or utilizing the quadratic formula $\frac{-b \pm \sqrt{b^2 - 4ac}}{2a}$ to derive the roots. These algebraic skills are directly applicable to the analysis of electrical waveforms, facilitating the identification and resolution of circuit anomalies and ensuring the stability of electrical systems.

The Reading Comprehension section is designed to evaluate a candidate's ability to effectively process, interpret, and critically analyze written information, a skill of paramount importance for understanding technical documents, operation manuals, and safety protocols within the electrical domain. Candidates are presented with passages followed by questions that scrutinize their grasp of the main ideas, the extraction of supporting details, and the discernment of the author's purpose. This section also tests the ability to make logical inferences, drawing conclusions based on the information presented, and to comprehend technical terminology within its given context. Success in this section necessitates the implementation of active reading strategies, which include identifying and underlining key points, annotating margins with brief notes, and summarizing paragraphs to reinforce understanding and retention of the technical material. These strategies enhance the candidate's ability to synthesize complex information and apply it effectively in real-world scenarios within the electrical field.

Test Structure & Scoring

Timing and Questions

The IBEW Aptitude Test is meticulously designed to evaluate candidates' abilities under the constraints of time, mirroring the high-stakes environment typical in electrical work scenarios. The examination is divided into two distinct sections: Algebra & Functions and Reading Comprehension, each with a strict time allocation that compels candidates to not only comprehend the material thoroughly but also to apply their understanding with precision and swiftness. The test comprises multiple-choice questions, a format that demands a methodical and tactical approach. Candidates are advised to develop proficiency in this format, enabling them to efficiently eliminate incorrect responses and concentrate on the most plausible options.

Within the Algebra & Functions section, candidates are presented with questions that span a spectrum from fundamental algebraic operations to intricate problems involving quadratic equations and linear functions. For instance, when addressing a linear equation of the form $y = mx + b$, candidates must adeptly manipulate the equation to isolate the variable y, accurately calculate the slope m, and precisely identify the y-intercept b. Mastery of solving quadratic equations, exemplified by $ax^2 + bx + c = 0$, is essential, particularly through the application of the quadratic formula $\frac{-b \pm \sqrt{b^2 - 4ac}}{2a}$. Engaging in extensive practice of these equations is vital for enhancing both speed and precision, enabling candidates to discern patterns that facilitate more rapid solutions.

In the Reading Comprehension section, the ability to manage time effectively is of paramount importance. Candidates must read passages with efficiency, skillfully identifying key ideas, supporting details, and the author's purpose without being hindered by complex vocabulary or convoluted sentence structures. Employing techniques such as skimming to capture main ideas and scanning to locate specific information can significantly bolster the ability to answer questions accurately while under the pressure of time constraints. Regularly practicing these reading strategies across a diverse range of texts cultivates the necessary skills to swiftly analyze passages and answer related questions with confidence.

Passing Score

Achieving a passing score on the IBEW Aptitude Test is a critical requirement for candidates aspiring to enter the electrical trade through an apprenticeship program. The test is designed to rigorously assess a candidate's preparedness for the demanding challenges of an apprenticeship by focusing specifically on essential mathematical and reading skills. Candidates are required to meet or exceed the minimum score threshold established by the International Brotherhood of Electrical Workers (IBEW), which is determined by each local union. This threshold generally corresponds to a set of competency standards that emphasize a solid understanding of algebraic principles and reading comprehension capabilities.

In the Algebra & Functions section of the test, candidates are expected to demonstrate proficiency in solving linear equations of the form $y = mx + b$, where m represents the slope and b the y-intercept, as well as quadratic equations expressed as $ax^2 + bx + c = 0$. Mastery of the quadratic formula $\frac{-b \pm \sqrt{b^2 - 4ac}}{2a}$ is essential, as it allows candidates to accurately determine the roots of quadratic equations. Additionally, candidates must be adept at manipulating algebraic expressions to isolate and solve for unknown variables—skills that are directly applicable to real-world electrical engineering problems. For instance, calculating electrical load involves determining the total power consumption of a circuit, while analyzing circuit behavior requires understanding how changes in variables affect the overall system.

In the Reading Comprehension section, candidates' success hinges on their ability to rapidly process and interpret technical passages. This involves identifying the main idea, which is the central concept or argument presented by the author, as well as extracting supporting details that provide evidence or elaboration on the main idea. Understanding the author's purpose, whether it is to inform, persuade, or explain, is also crucial. Employing active reading strategies, such as annotating the text with notes or highlighting key points, and summarizing paragraphs in one's own words, can significantly enhance comprehension and retention. These skills are vital for accurately answering questions under the pressure of timed conditions, where efficiency and precision are paramount.

To optimize their scoring potential, candidates should engage in targeted practice that closely simulates the test environment. This involves taking timed quizzes that replicate the format and difficulty level of the actual exam, with a particular focus on addressing areas of weakness identified through self-assessment or practice test results. Utilizing resources such as algebra refresher courses can provide structured opportunities to reinforce mathematical skills, while reading comprehension workshops can offer strategies to improve understanding and interpretation of complex texts. These preparatory activities are designed to enhance the candidate's overall performance on the test, ensuring they possess the requisite skills to succeed in the electrical trade.

When You'll Get Results

Following the completion of the IBEW Aptitude Test, candidates enter a period of anticipation as they await their results, which are typically released within several weeks. This interval is not arbitrary; it is deliberately designed to allow for a meticulous and thorough evaluation of each individual test. The evaluation process involves a detailed analysis of the responses provided by each candidate, ensuring that every aspect of their performance is accurately assessed and that the resulting scores reflect their true capabilities. Understanding the intricacies of this scoring process can alleviate some of the anxiety candidates may experience during this waiting period.

The scoring mechanism of the IBEW Aptitude Test is structured to assess proficiency in critical areas deemed essential for success in the electrical trade. The test is divided into distinct sections: one focusing on Algebra & Functions and the other on Reading Comprehension. Each section is evaluated independently, yielding separate scores that reflect the candidate's ability in those specific domains. Subsequently, these individual scores are integrated to form a composite score, which serves as a comprehensive indicator of the candidate's overall performance. The International Brotherhood of Electrical Workers (IBEW) establishes a minimum passing score threshold, which varies according to the specific requirements of each local union. Meeting or exceeding this score is a pivotal step for candidates aspiring to progress in the apprenticeship application process, as it is often a prerequisite for further consideration.

Upon the conclusion of the scoring process, candidates are notified of their results through the communication method designated by their testing location. This may include electronic mail, traditional postal services, or direct communication facilitated by the local union. It is imperative for candidates to ensure that their contact information is current and accurate, and they should consistently monitor their email inbox, including checking spam or junk folders, to prevent missing any crucial notifications regarding their test results.

In instances where candidates do not achieve the desired outcome, there is generally an opportunity to retake the test after a specified waiting period, which varies depending on the location. This interval serves as an opportune time for candidates to engage in a thorough review of the test material, with a particular emphasis on areas where they encountered difficulties. Utilizing resources such as practice tests, comprehensive study guides, and targeted educational courses can significantly enhance their understanding and improve their performance in future attempts.

Candidates who successfully achieve a passing score typically advance to subsequent stages of the apprenticeship application process, which may include interviews or additional assessments. Securing a high score on the IBEW Aptitude Test is indicative of a candidate's preparedness for the demanding nature of an electrical apprenticeship and sets a favorable precedent for the ensuing steps in the application journey.

Chapter 1:
Number Properties and Operations

1.1: Types and Behavior of Numbers

Types of Numbers

A comprehensive understanding of the various classifications of numbers is crucial for effectively navigating the mathematical concepts encountered in the IBEW Aptitude Test. Numbers are systematically categorized into distinct groups: integers, rational numbers, irrational numbers, and real numbers. Each group is defined by specific properties that are integral to the resolution of diverse algebraic challenges.

Integers, denoted by the symbol $\mathbf{Z}$, encompass all whole numbers. This includes the entire set of positive numbers (e.g., *1, 2, 3*), negative numbers (e.g., *-1, -2, -3*), and zero. It is important to note that integers do not include any fractional or decimal components. For instance, the number *-2* is an integer, as it is a whole number without any decimal or fractional part. Similarly, zero, represented as 0, is a neutral integer that plays a pivotal role in arithmetic operations as the additive identity.

Rational numbers are those that can be precisely expressed as the quotient $\frac{p}{q}$ of two integers, where p is the numerator and q is the non-zero denominator. The set of rational numbers is symbolized by $\cdot$. This category is inclusive of integers, since any integer z can be rewritten as $\frac{z}{1}$. Rational numbers also encompass fractions such as $\frac{1}{2}$ which represents the division of the integer *1* by the integer *2*. Additionally, rational numbers include decimals that either terminate, like 0.75, which can be converted to the fraction $\frac{75}{100}$, or repeat indefinitely, such as 0,3, which is equivalent to $\frac{1}{3}$.

Irrational numbers are characterized by their inability to be represented as a simple fraction $\frac{p}{q}$. These numbers manifest as non-repeating, non-terminating decimals. A classic example is $\sqrt{2}$, which cannot be accurately expressed as a fraction of two integers and has a decimal expansion that neither terminates nor repeats. Similarly, the number π , approximately

3.14159, is an irrational number with a decimal representation that continues infinitely without a repeating pattern. The mathematical constant e , approximately 2.71828, also belongs to this category. The symbol I is used to denote irrational numbers.

Real numbers, represented by the symbol $\mathbb{R}$, include both rational and irrational numbers, thus forming a complete set that corresponds to every conceivable point on an infinite number line. Real numbers are distinct from imaginary numbers, which involve the square root of negative one and do not fall within the real number continuum. The real number system provides a comprehensive framework for representing and analyzing numerical values that are encountered in various mathematical contexts.

Understanding these distinctions is essential for the IBEW Aptitude Test. When engaging with algebraic equations or analyzing functions, determining whether a solution is an integer, rational, or irrational is crucial for guiding the problem-solving strategy. Real numbers are the predominant type encountered, serving as the basis for most mathematical operations required in the test. Proficiency in identifying these types of numbers and their inherent properties will significantly enhance one's ability to effectively address the algebra and functions section.

Even, Odd, and Prime Numbers

Understanding the properties and characteristics of even, odd, and prime numbers is essential for addressing a diverse array of mathematical challenges, such as those encountered on the IBEW Aptitude Test. These concepts serve as foundational elements within arithmetic and play a pivotal role in executing algebraic operations and navigating problem-solving contexts.

Even numbers constitute a subset of integers defined by their divisibility by the integer 2, yielding a quotient that is an integer and a remainder of zero. Formally, an integer n is classified as even if it satisfies the equation $n = 2k$, where k represents any integer, including positive and negative values as well as zero. For example, the integer *2* can be expressed as *2 × 1*, the integer *4* as *2 × 2*, and the integer *-6* as *2 × (-3)*. These expressions illustrate the fundamental property that defines even numbers. When two even numbers are subjected to addition, such as *2 + 4*, the result is another even number, specifically *6*, which can be expressed as *2 × 3*. Similarly, subtracting two even numbers, such as *4 – 2*, yields *2*, which is also even. Multiplying an even number by any integer, for instance, *4 × 3*, results in *12*, another even number, which can be represented as *2 × 6*.

Odd numbers, in contrast, are integers that do not fulfill the divisibility criteria for the integer *2*, resulting in a remainder of 1 when divided by 2. An odd number n can be mathematically represented as $n = 2k + 1$, where k is an integer. For instance, the number *3* can be expressed as *2 × 1 + 1*, the number *-5* as *2 × (-3) +1*, and the number *7* as *2 × 3 + 1*. These representations highlight the inherent nature of odd numbers. When two odd numbers are added, such as *3 + 5*, the sum is *8*, an even number, which can be expressed as 2 x 4. Subtracting two odd numbers, such as *7 – 3*, results in *4*, which is also even. Multiplying two odd numbers, for example, *3 x 5*, yields *15*, an odd number, which can be expressed as *2 x 7 + 1*.

Prime numbers are defined as integers greater than 1 that possess the unique property of having exactly two distinct positive divisors: 1 and the number itself. Examples of prime numbers include *2*, *3*, *5*, *7*, and *11*. It is noteworthy that *2* holds the distinction of being the only even prime number, as all other prime numbers are odd due to their indivisibility by *2*. A profound understanding of prime numbers is critical for the factorization of composite numbers and the resolution of various algebraic expressions. When a prime number is multiplied by any integer, such as when multiplying *3* by *4*, the resultant product is a composite number, in this case, *12*, which can be factored into *2 x 2 x 3*.

Divisibility Rules

Divisibility rules serve as essential computational techniques for swiftly determining whether one integer can be divided by another without leaving a remainder, a proficiency crucial in both routine arithmetic operations and in the context of the IBEW Aptitude Test. These rules streamline the divisibility verification process, allowing individuals to tackle a diverse array of mathematical problems with increased efficiency, thus mitigating the need for the cumbersome process of long division.

To ascertain if a number is divisible by 2, one must inspect the number's final digit and confirm if it belongs to the set of even numerals, specifically *0*, *2*, *4*, *6*, or *8*. This criterion hinges on the fundamental property of even numbers, which are inherently divisible by 2. For instance, consider the integer *146*; its terminal digit is *6*, an even number, thereby confirming that *146* is divisible by *2*.

When evaluating divisibility by *3*, the procedure involves summing all individual digits of the number and assessing whether the resulting total is divisible by *3*. This method leverages the property that a number is divisible by 3 if and only if the sum of its digits shares this divisibility. For example, with the number *231*, the calculation proceeds as follows: *2 + 3 + 1 = 6*. Since *6* is divisible by *3*, it follows that *231* is also divisible by *3*.

To determine divisibility by *4*, one must focus on the number constituted by the last two digits of the entire number. If this two-digit number is divisible by *4*, then the original number is confirmed to be divisible by *4*. For instance, examine *1324*; the last two digits form the number *24*. Since *24* divided by *4* yields an integer, *1324* is confirmed to be divisible by *4*.

A number's divisibility by *5* can be swiftly verified by checking if its last digit is either a *0* or a *5*. This rule exploits the base-10 system, where multiples of *5* naturally end in these digits, thus providing a rapid method for excluding certain options in multiple-choice scenarios.

To ascertain divisibility by *6*, a number must satisfy the conditions for divisibility by both *2* and *3* simultaneously. For example, consider the number *48*; it meets the criteria for divisibility by *2*, as it ends in the even digit *8*. Additionally, the sum of its digits, *4 + 8 = 12*, is divisible by *3*. Hence, *48* is divisible by *6*, as it satisfies both requisite conditions.

The rule for divisibility by *9* necessitates that the sum of a number's digits itself be divisible by *9*. This is predicated on the fact that a number is divisible by *9* if and only if the sum of its digits is divisible by *9*. For instance, the number *198* has digits that sum to *18*, and since *18* is divisible by *9*, it follows that *198* is divisible by *9*.

A number's divisibility by *10* is confirmed if it terminates in the digit *0*. This straightforward rule is a direct consequence of the decimal system, where multiples of *10* consistently end in *0*, facilitating an immediate determination of divisibility by *10*.

1.2: Core Mathematical Laws

Commutative, Associative, Distributive Laws

Understanding the commutative, associative, and distributive laws is essential for effectively addressing complex mathematical problems, particularly those encountered on the IBEW aptitude test. These fundamental principles form the foundation of algebraic operations, enabling the transformation and simplification of expressions as well as the resolution of equations with accuracy.

The commutative law, applicable to both addition and multiplication, specifies that the order in which two numbers are added or multiplied does not influence the final result. For any two real numbers *a* and *b*, this principle is articulated as *a + b = b + a* for addition and *ab = ba* for multiplication. For instance, consider the operation *3 + 7*, which yields the same sum as *7 + 3*, thus demonstrating the interchangeable nature of the operands. Similarly, the product *4 × 5* is equivalent to *5 × 4*, confirming that the sequence of factors can be rearranged without affecting the product. This property proves particularly advantageous in computational contexts, where restructuring terms can streamline the calculation process.

The associative law asserts that the manner in which numbers are grouped during addition or multiplication does not affect the outcome. This law is formally expressed as *(a + b) + c = a + (b + c)* for addition and *(ab)c = a(bc)* for multiplication. To illustrate, whether one computes *2 + (3 + 4)* or rearranges it as *(2 + 3) + 4*, the result remains consistent, exemplifying the law's utility in maintaining the integrity of sums despite regrouping. Similarly, for multiplication, the expression *2(3 × 4)* can be restructured to *2 × 3 × 4*, yielding the same product. This capability is essential when addressing intricate equations, as it allows for the strategic grouping of terms, which can significantly simplify the computational workload.

The distributive law establishes a relationship between addition and multiplication, providing a method to multiply a single term by a sum or difference within parentheses. This law is expressed as $a(b + c) = ab + ac$ and $a(b - c) = ab - ac$. It serves as a powerful tool for expanding expressions and managing equations involving parentheses. For example, to simplify the expression $3(2 + 4)$, the distributive law is applied to yield $3 \times 2 + 3 \times 4 = 6 + 12 = 18$, demonstrating how multiplication can be distributed over addition to facilitate calculation.

These algebraic laws enable the transformation of expressions into equivalent forms that are more conducive to manipulation and simplification. For instance, when tasked with solving an equation such as $x + 3 = 5$, a thorough understanding of these laws is instrumental in isolating the variable x. By subtracting 3 from both sides of the equation, one can utilize the commutative and associative laws to ensure that the equation remains balanced, ultimately simplifying the process of solving for x.

Identity and Inverse Properties

A comprehensive understanding of both the identity and inverse properties is indispensable for achieving proficiency in the foundational concepts of algebra, which are pivotal for success in the IBEW aptitude test. These mathematical properties are instrumental in the simplification of algebraic expressions and the efficient resolution of equations, serving as the bedrock for more advanced problem-solving techniques.

The identity property of addition is defined by the principle that the sum of zero and any given number will result in the original number remaining unchanged. This can be formally expressed with the equation $a + 0 = a$, where a represents any real number. In a similar fashion, the identity property of multiplication stipulates that the product of any number and one yields the original number, as denoted by the equation $a \times 1 = a$. These properties are fundamental in maintaining the structural integrity and consistency of numerical systems across various operations, thereby ensuring that basic arithmetic operations do not alter the inherent value of the numbers involved.

Inverse properties pertain to operations that effectively return a number to its original state through the application of complementary operations. The additive inverse property involves the addition of a number to its additive opposite, or negative counterpart, resulting in a sum of zero, as illustrated by the equation $a + (-a) = 0$. This property is particularly crucial in the context of solving algebraic equations, as it facilitates the elimination of specific terms to isolate and solve for variables. The multiplicative inverse, commonly referred to as the reciprocal, involves multiplying a number by its reciprocal such that the product is one, represented by

$a \times \dfrac{1}{a} = 1$, with the stipulation that a must not be zero to prevent undefined operations. This

principle is especially advantageous when solving equations that necessitate division by a variable, enabling the simplification and resolution of more complex expressions.

To illustrate the application of these concepts, consider the expression $3 + 0$. By employing the identity property of addition, this expression is simplified to 3, thereby demonstrating that the addition of zero does not alter the value of the original number. Similarly, in the equation $x \times 1 = x$, the identity property of multiplication affirms that the variable x retains its original value, as the multiplication by one does not affect the outcome.

Analyzing the process of solving an equation such as $x + 5 = 5$ involves the application of the additive inverse property. By subtracting 5 from both sides of the equation, the additive inverse property is utilized to isolate the variable, resulting in the simplified equation $x = 0$. In a scenario requiring division, consider the equation $4x = 8$. By multiplying both sides by the multiplicative inverse of 4, which is expressed as $\frac{1}{4}$, the equation is simplified to $x = 2$. This demonstrates the utility of the multiplicative inverse in transforming the equation into a solvable form, thereby highlighting its importance in algebraic manipulation and problem-solving.

Chapter 2: Basic Arithmetic Skills

2.1: Efficient Calculation Techniques

Addition & Subtraction Shortcuts

Mastering mental arithmetic for addition and subtraction is essential for enhancing computational speed, a critical skill for those preparing for the IBEW aptitude test. This discussion delves into specific techniques that leverage numerical properties to facilitate rapid mental calculations.

Rounding and Adjusting

An effective mental arithmetic technique involves rounding numbers to the nearest ten, hundred, or thousand, depending on their magnitude, followed by precise adjustments to the final result. Consider the operation of adding *198 + 467*. First, round *198* to the nearest hundred, resulting in *200*, and round *467* to *500*. The sum of these rounded numbers is *700*. Next, calculate the deviation from the original numbers: *198* is *2* less than *200* and *467* is *33* less than *500*. Therefore, the combined deviation is *–2 –33 = –35*. Subtract this deviation from the rounded sum: *700 – 35 = 665*. This method efficiently simplifies the arithmetic by minimizing cognitive load and reducing potential errors.

Breaking Down Numbers

Breaking numbers into manageable components is another method that simplifies addition and subtraction. When tasked with subtracting *456 – 112*, decompose *112* into *100 + 12*. First, subtract *100* from *456* , resulting in *356*. Then, subtract the remaining *12* from *356* to achieve the final result of *344*. This process, known as decomposition, leverages the ease of subtracting round numbers, allowing for straightforward mental calculations by reducing complex operations into simpler steps.

Using Complements

The use of complements is particularly advantageous in subtraction scenarios. A complement of a number is the amount needed to reach the next whole ten, hundred, or similar benchmark. For example, the complement of *4* in the context of *10* is *6*, since *4 + 6 = 10*. When subtracting *9* from *23*, recognize that *9* is *1* less than *10*. Subtract *10* from *23* to get *13*, and then add back the that was subtracted in excess, resulting in *14*. This technique effectively transforms subtraction into a simpler addition task.

Doubling and Halving

In scenarios involving both addition and subtraction, identifying opportunities to double one number while halving the other can simplify the calculation, especially when one number is even. For instance, instead of directly adding *8 + 150*, halve *8* to *4* and double *150* to *300*. This transforms the calculation into a simpler operation: *4 + 300 = 304*. This method is particularly useful for mental calculations as it leverages the properties of numbers to reduce the complexity of the arithmetic involved.

Close Multiples

When dealing with numbers that are numerically close to each other, utilizing their average and making necessary adjustments can simplify the calculation. For example, when adding *199 + 202*, observe that both numbers are near *200*. Calculate their average, which is *200.5*. Since the task involves adding two numbers, double the average to obtain *401*. This approach reduces the cognitive burden by focusing on the central value and adjusting accordingly, streamlining the mental arithmetic process.

Multiplication & Division Strategies

Mastering the operations of multiplication and division with multi-digit numbers is a critical skill for individuals preparing for the IBEW aptitude test, as it demands not only an understanding of mathematical concepts but also the ability to execute these operations with precision and speed. This section delves into specific strategies designed to optimize these operations, emphasizing the importance of both efficiency and accuracy to enhance your mathematical capabilities.

In the context of multiplication, the traditional algorithm, often referred to as long multiplication, requires a systematic approach whereby each digit of the multiplicand (the bottom number) is multiplied sequentially by each digit of the multiplier (the top number). This process involves generating partial products that are subsequently summed to yield the final result. However, when dealing with numbers that contain a large number of digits, this method can become labor-intensive and prone to errors. An alternative approach is the lattice method, which reformulates multiplication into a structured grid format. This method involves constructing a grid where each cell corresponds to a single-digit multiplication. The multiplicand and multiplier are aligned along the top and right side of the grid, respectively. Each intersection within the grid is divided diagonally, creating two triangular sections. The results of the single-digit multiplications are placed within these sections, with the tens digit in the upper triangle and the units digit in the lower triangle. The final product is computed by summing the numbers along the diagonals of the grid, commencing from the bottom right corner. This technique not only simplifies the process but also minimizes potential calculation errors by compartmentalizing each multiplication step.

Another multiplication technique, particularly advantageous when dealing with numbers that are close to powers of ten, leverages the algebraic identity known as the difference of squares, expressed as *(a + b)(a − b) = a² − b²*. To illustrate, consider the task of multiplying *98* by *102*. This can be reinterpreted as *(100 − 2)(100 + 2)*, allowing the problem to be simplified using the identity. Here, *a* is *100* and *b* is 2, transforming the multiplication into *100² − 2²*. Calculating *100²* yields *10000*, and *2²* results in *4*. Subtracting these *gives 10000 − 4 = 9996*. This method circumvents the need for traditional multiplication by utilizing a mathematical shortcut that capitalizes on the properties of numbers near base powers, thereby streamlining the calculation process.

When simplifying division, particularly with multi-digit divisors, it is essential to grasp and apply the principles of long division by decomposing the process into a series of manageable steps. For division involving substantial numbers, an effective strategy is to estimate and round the divisor to a nearby, more straightforward number, facilitating an easier division. As an example, when faced with dividing *12345* by *98*, one might round *98* to *100*, simplifying the division to *123.45*. This estimation provides an initial quotient, which can then be refined to achieve greater precision by adjusting for the rounding.

Prime factorization serves as a powerful tool in the simplification of calculations for both multiplication and division. By decomposing numbers into their constituent prime factors, one can streamline the simplification of fractions and enhance the manageability of division involving large numbers. This is achieved by identifying and canceling out common factors between the numerator and the denominator, thereby reducing the complexity of the calculation and yielding a simplified result.

2.2: Estimation and Mixed Practice

Estimation and Rounding

Estimation and rounding serve as critical mathematical techniques, particularly in the preparation for the IBEW aptitude test, where they function as indispensable tools to streamline complex calculations and facilitate a rapid verification process for ensuring the precision of detailed computational work. To employ estimation effectively, it is imperative to possess a thorough understanding of the principles governing the rounding of numbers. This involves adjusting numbers to the nearest ten, hundred, or thousand, a decision that is contingent upon the specific context and requirements of the problem at hand. Mastery of this skill necessitates a deep comprehension of the positional value of each digit within a number, recognizing how each digit influences the overall magnitude and contributes to the number's total value.

For instance, when tasked with estimating the sum or difference of large numerical values, the process is significantly simplified by rounding each number to a meaningful digit prior to performing the arithmetic operation. Take the task of estimating the sum of and as an example. By rounding *2,453* upward to *2,500* and *1,678* to *1,700*, the complexity of the operation is reduced to a straightforward addition of *2,500* + *1,700*, yielding an estimated sum of *4,200*. This approach is particularly advantageous in test scenarios where time efficiency is paramount, and achieving a close approximation is prioritized over obtaining an exact numerical result.

Moreover, rounding is integral in evaluating the plausibility of results derived from more detailed and precise computational methods. After resolving a complex mathematical problem, employing estimation allows for a rapid assessment of whether the detailed solution lies within a plausible range. For example, if a meticulous calculation produces a result of *4,132*, and a preliminary estimation suggests a value in the vicinity of *4,200*, the closeness of these figures offers immediate reassurance regarding the accuracy of the initial calculation.

Within the context of the IBEW aptitude test, the ability to adeptly utilize estimation and rounding provides candidates with a strategic edge. This capability enables them to manage their time with greater efficiency, allowing for swift verification of their work while furnishing them with a method to address complex mathematical challenges with increased speed and confidence. Developing proficiency in this skill effectively transforms it into a potent tool, equipping candidates to navigate the mathematical demands of the test with enhanced competence.

Mixed Operations

Handling mixed operations necessitates a precise application of addition, subtraction, multiplication, and division in a sequential manner to address multi-step problems that require a systematic approach. This proficiency is crucial for the IBEW aptitude test, as it reflects the intricate nature of electrical calculations encountered in practical scenarios, where accuracy and methodical problem-solving are essential.

To effectively solve a problem involving mixed operations, it is imperative to first identify and adhere to the established order of operations, encapsulated by the acronym PEMDAS. This mnemonic device represents Parentheses, Exponents, Multiplication and Division (performed from left to right in the sequence they appear), and Addition and Subtraction (also executed from left to right). Adhering to this hierarchy guarantees that each mathematical operation is carried out in the correct sequence, thereby yielding an accurate result.

Consider the example problem $8 + 2 \times (15 - 5) \div 5$. The initial step involves addressing the operation contained within the parentheses:

1. Calculate the expression inside the parentheses by subtracting *5* from *15*, resulting in *10*.
2. Proceed by multiplying *2* by the result obtained, *10*, to arrive at *20*. Subsequently, divide this product by *5* to obtain *4*.
3. Finally, add *8* to the quotient *4*, culminating in the final solution, which is *12*.

This problem-solving approach underscores the importance of methodically dissecting complex equations into manageable components, solving each part in a step-by-step manner.

In scenarios involving more intricate problems that include variables, the same foundational principles apply, supplemented by algebraic manipulation techniques. For instance, to determine the value of x in the equation $4x + 2 = 2(x + 5)$, begin with distribution and then simplify the expression:

1. Distribute the coefficient 2 across the terms within the parentheses, transforming the equation into $4x + 2 = 2x + 10$.
2. Rearrange the terms to isolate the variable x by subtracting $2x$ from both sides, resulting in the simplified equation $4x - 2x = 10 - 2$.
3. Simplify the resulting expression to $2x = 8$, and solve for x by dividing both sides by 2, yielding $x = 4$.

Achieving mastery in mixed operations necessitates consistent practice with a diverse array of problem types to develop fluency in transitioning seamlessly between different operations. Additionally, employing estimation techniques serves as a valuable tool for verifying the plausibility of solutions. For example, estimating that multiplying 2 by 10 results in 20, and dividing 20 by 5 yields 4, suggests that adding should produce a sum near 12, thus corroborating the accuracy of the computed answer.

Chapter 3: Fractions and Decimals

3.1: Understanding and Converting

Fraction Basics

Understanding the intricacies of fractions is crucial for candidates preparing for the IBEW aptitude test, as these mathematical elements constitute the foundation of numerous problems encountered both in the examination and throughout the electrical trade. A fraction is a mathematical expression denoting the division of a whole into smaller, equal segments, represented by two distinct components: the numerator and the denominator. The numerator, positioned above the horizontal fraction bar, quantifies the number of specific segments of the whole that are being considered, while the denominator, situated below the fraction bar, delineates the total number of equal segments into which the whole is divided.

Fractions can be classified into several distinct categories, each serving unique mathematical functions. Proper fractions are characterized by a numerator that is numerically less than the denominator, symbolizing a quantity that is less than a single unit. Conversely, improper fractions possess a numerator that is either equal to or exceeds the denominator, indicating a quantity that is equal to or surpasses a single unit. Mixed numbers, which combine a whole number and a proper fraction, are utilized to express quantities greater than a singular unit.

The ability to convert between mixed numbers and improper fractions is a critical skill that simplifies mathematical computations. To convert a mixed number into an improper fraction, one must first multiply the whole number component by the denominator of the fractional part, then add the numerator of the fractional part to this product, and finally place the resultant sum over the original denominator. For instance, to convert the mixed number $3\frac{1}{4}$ into an improper fraction, calculate *3 x 4 + 1 = 13*, thereby resulting in the improper fraction $\frac{13}{4}$.

Conversely, to convert an improper fraction back into a mixed number, one must perform a division of the numerator by the denominator to ascertain the whole number component, with the remainder from this division becoming the numerator of the fractional component. For example, converting the improper fraction $\frac{13}{4}$ back into a mixed number involves dividing *13* by *4*, which yields a quotient of *3* and a remainder of *1*, thus resulting in the mixed number $3\frac{1}{4}$.

Acquiring proficiency in these fundamental operations equips candidates with the confidence to address more intricate mathematical challenges. Skills such as comparing fractions, identifying common denominators, and converting between mixed numbers and improper fractions are vital. The ability to recognize and manipulate various fractional representations enhances one's proficiency in interpreting and resolving a broad spectrum of mathematical problems, thereby establishing a robust foundation for success on the IBEW aptitude test and in subsequent electrical work.

Fraction-Decimal Conversion

The conversion between fractions and decimals represents an essential skill for candidates preparing for the IBEW aptitude test, as it enables them to efficiently manage a variety of mathematical challenges. This process relies on the understanding that fractions and decimals are two distinct formats for expressing the same quantitative concept: a segment of a whole entity. When converting a fraction into its decimal form, the procedure involves dividing the numerator, which is the upper component of the fraction, by the denominator, the lower component. For instance, to transform the fraction $\frac{3}{4}$ into a decimal, one must execute the division operation of *3* by *4*, resulting in *0.75*. This division-based method is universally applicable to any fraction, irrespective of its numerical complexity or size.

In the reverse process of translating decimals into fractions, it is crucial to first ascertain the place value of the decimal number to accurately determine an appropriate denominator. Take, for example, the decimal *0.75*, which can be interpreted as representing *75* out of *100* parts, thereby forming the fraction $\frac{75}{100}$. To simplify this fraction, one must identify the greatest common divisor (GCD) of the numerator and the denominator, which in this case is *25*. By dividing both the numerator and denominator by this GCD, the fraction simplifies to $\frac{3}{4}$.

Possessing immediate recognition of frequently encountered fractions and their corresponding decimal forms can greatly enhance efficiency and minimize the likelihood of errors. Familiarity with the fact that $\frac{1}{2}$ equates to *0.5*, $\frac{1}{4}$ corresponds to *0.25*, and $\frac{3}{4}$ matches *0.75* enables swift conversions without the necessity of performing division calculations. This pre-existing knowledge is particularly beneficial in the context of a timed test environment where rapid and accurate processing is essential.

When addressing fractions that yield repeating decimal sequences, such as $\frac{1}{3}$, which results in a decimal representation of *0.333...*, it is vital to recognize that these can be approximated to a desired level of precision, such as *0.33*, contingent upon the specific requirements of the problem at hand. This practice of rounding aligns with the test's emphasis on pragmatic problem-solving and real-world applications, where the need for absolute precision is often secondary to a comprehensive grasp of the underlying concepts and their practical utilization.

3.2: Fraction and Decimal Operations

Add, Subtract, Multiply, Divide Fractions

To add fractions, initiate the process by identifying a common denominator, which serves as a shared base for the fractions involved. For the fractions $\frac{1}{4}$ and $\frac{1}{3}$, calculate the least common multiple (LCM) of the denominators 4 and 3. The LCM of these two numbers is 12, as it is the smallest number that both denominators divide into without leaving a remainder. Next, convert each fraction to an equivalent fraction with this common denominator. For $\frac{1}{4}$, multiply both the numerator and the denominator by 3, resulting in $\frac{3}{12}$. Similarly, for $\frac{1}{3}$, multiply both the numerator and the denominator by 4, yielding $\frac{4}{12}$. With the fractions now possessing a common denominator, proceed to add the numerators directly: $3 + 4 = 7$. The sum is $\frac{7}{12}$, with the denominator remaining unchanged.

Subtraction of fractions employs a parallel methodology. To subtract $\frac{2}{5}$ from $\frac{3}{4}$, first ascertain the least common denominator, which is the LCM of 4 and 5. The LCM here is 20. Convert $\frac{3}{4}$ to an equivalent fraction with a denominator of 20 by multiplying both the numerator and the denominator by 5, resulting in $\frac{15}{20}$. For $\frac{2}{5}$, multiply both the numerator and the denominator by 4, obtaining $\frac{8}{20}$. With equivalent denominators established, subtract the numerators: $15 - 8 = 7$, resulting in $\frac{7}{20}$, where the denominator remains constant.

When multiplying fractions, the operation involves multiplying the numerators and the denominators directly across. For the multiplication of $\frac{3}{4}$ by $\frac{2}{5}$, calculate the product of the numerators: $3 \times 2 = 6$. Concurrently, compute the product of the denominators: $4 \times 5 = 20$. This results in the fraction $\frac{6}{20}$. Simplify this fraction by identifying and dividing by the greatest common divisor (GCD) of *6* and *20*, which is *2*, yielding $\frac{3}{10}$.

Dividing fractions involves taking the reciprocal of the second fraction and then performing multiplication. To divide $\frac{3}{4}$ by $\frac{2}{5}$, first find the reciprocal of $\frac{2}{5}$, which is $\frac{5}{2}$. Then, multiply $\frac{3}{4}$ by $\frac{5}{2}$. Multiply the numerators: *3 × 5 = 15*, and the denominators: *4 × 2 = 8*, resulting in *8*.

For efficiency and accuracy in operations:
- When denominators are identical for addition or subtraction, directly perform the operation on the numerators, maintaining the common denominator.
- Employ the least common multiple (LCM) to streamline the process of finding a common denominator, ensuring minimal computational complexity.
- Prior to multiplication, simplify by canceling any common factors between numerators and denominators across fractions, thereby reducing the fractions to their simplest form to prevent unnecessary calculations.
- The mnemonic "Keep, Change, Flip" aids in division: retain the first fraction as is, alter the division operation to multiplication, and invert the second fraction to its reciprocal.

Engage with this practice problem to solidify understanding:

For addition, identify the least common denominator (LCD) between $\frac{5}{8}$ and $\frac{1}{6}$, which is *24*. Convert each fraction: $\frac{5}{8} = \frac{15}{24}$ and $\frac{1}{6} = \frac{4}{24}$. Add: $\frac{15}{24} + \frac{4}{24} = \frac{19}{24}$.

For subtraction, the LCD for $\frac{7}{9}$ and $\frac{2}{3}$ is *9*. Convert: $\frac{2}{3} = \frac{6}{9}$. Subtract: $\frac{7}{9} - \frac{6}{9} = \frac{1}{9}$.

For multiplication, calculate $\frac{3}{7} \times \frac{4}{5}$ directly, resulting in $\frac{12}{35}$, with no further simplification necessary.

For division, apply "Keep, Change, Flip": $\frac{4}{9} \times \frac{3}{2}$ results in $\frac{12}{18}$, simplifying to $\frac{2}{3}$ by dividing both the numerator and the denominator by their GCD, which is *6*.

Decimal Operations

Executing arithmetic operations with decimal numbers requires meticulous attention to detail and a comprehensive understanding of the concept of place value. In the context of adding or subtracting decimals, it is imperative to ensure that the decimal points of the numbers involved are aligned vertically. This alignment guarantees that each digit is positioned correctly within its respective place value column, which is crucial for maintaining accuracy in the calculation. For instance, consider the task of adding the decimal numbers *3.75* and *2.1*. Begin by writing the numbers in a column, ensuring that the decimal points are directly aligned one above the other:

$$3.75 +$$
$$\underline{2.10 =}$$
$$5.85$$

Observe that the number *2.1* has fewer decimal places than *3.75*. To address this discrepancy, append a zero to *2.1*, transforming it into *2.10*. This zero serves no numerical value but is essential for maintaining uniformity across the decimal places, thereby ensuring that the addition process is executed correctly.

When approaching the multiplication of decimal numbers, the focus should be on the cumulative count of decimal places present in both multiplicands. The multiplication process can be simplified by initially disregarding the decimal points and treating the numbers as integers. Take, for example, the multiplication of *3.2* by *0,5*. First, convert these decimals into whole numbers by removing the decimal points, resulting in *32* and *5*, respectively. Proceed by multiplying these integers to obtain a product of *160*. Subsequently, reintroduce the decimal point into the product. Since the original numbers *3.2* and *0,5* each contain one decimal place, the product must reflect a total of two decimal places. By counting two places from the right, the decimal is positioned between the *1* and *6*, yielding a final result of *1.60*, which can also be expressed as *1.6* without altering the value.

In the division of decimal numbers, the initial step involves transforming the divisor into a whole number by shifting its decimal point to the right. This shift must be mirrored in the dividend to maintain the equation's balance. Consider the division of *6.4* by *0,8*. Shift the decimal point in *0,8* one position to the right to convert it into *8*. Apply an identical shift to *6.4*, turning it into *64*. The division now simplifies to $64 \div 8$, resulting in a quotient of *8*.

Key Concepts for Decimal Operations:

- **Alignment for Addition/Subtraction:** Ensure decimal points are precisely aligned in a vertical manner to maintain each digit's position in its correct place value column.

- **Zero Padding:** Introduce zeros to the number with fewer decimal places to match the length of the other number, thereby facilitating accurate addition or subtraction.

- **Decimal Places in Multiplication:** Calculate the total number of decimal places by summing those in the multiplicands, and position the decimal in the product accordingly.

- **Adjusting Division:** Convert the divisor into a whole number by shifting its decimal point to the right, and apply the same adjustment to the dividend to preserve the integrity of the division operation.

Chapter 4: Exponents and Roots

4.1: Mastering Exponents

Basics and Notation

A comprehensive understanding of exponents is indispensable for delving into the intricacies of various mathematical concepts, particularly when preparing for the International Brotherhood of Electrical Workers (IBEW) aptitude test. An exponent comprises two integral components: the base and the exponent itself. The base serves as the central element that undergoes repeated multiplication by itself, whereas the exponent, positioned as a superscript to the right of the base, precisely dictates the number of times the base is utilized as a multiplicative factor in the operation.

Take, for instance, the expression 5^3. Here, the number 5 functions as the base, and the number 3 serves as the exponent. This mathematical expression indicates that the base, 5, is to be multiplied by itself a total of three times, leading to the computation $5 \times 5 \times 5$, which results in the product 125. The exponent serves as a compact notation to efficiently convey the concept of repeated multiplication, thereby streamlining complex calculations.

When dealing with negative exponents, the concept of division is introduced into the realm of exponents. A negative exponent signifies that the base is repositioned into the denominator of a fractional expression, with the numerator being 1. For example, the expression 5^{-3} is interpreted as $\frac{1}{5^3}$, which further simplifies to $\frac{1}{125}$. This notation provides a more efficient means to express division operations within algebraic contexts, facilitating the manipulation and simplification of expressions.

The case where zero is used as an exponent introduces a distinct rule: any non-zero base raised to the power of zero is equal to 1. This principle is articulated as $a^0 = 1$, where a represents any non-zero numerical value. This rule is pivotal for the simplification of expressions and plays a crucial role in solving equations that incorporate exponents, allowing for streamlined calculations and reducing potential computational complexities.

A thorough comprehension of the laws that govern exponent operations is equally important. Among these laws is the product of powers law, which permits the addition of exponents when multiplying two powers that share the same base: $a^m \times a^n = a^{m+n}$. This law is fundamental in simplifying expressions involving multiplication of similar bases. The quotient of powers law involves the subtraction of exponents when dividing two powers with an identical base: $a^m \div a^n = a^{m-n}$. This principle is crucial for simplifying division operations. The power of a power law states that when an exponent is raised to another exponent, the exponents are multiplied: $(a^m)^n = a^{m \times n}$. This law is essential for managing expressions where exponents are nested.

These foundational principles and the specific notation associated with exponents constitute the core of understanding algebraic operations, which is essential for addressing intricate problems on the IBEW aptitude test and in the professional practice of an electrician. Proficiency in the structure and operational laws of exponents provides the essential tools required to tackle a diverse array of mathematical challenges.

Exponent Rules Simplification

A comprehensive understanding of the rules governing exponents is imperative for the simplification of mathematical expressions, particularly when preparing to tackle the challenges presented by the IBEW aptitude test. These rules serve as essential tools that significantly enhance the efficiency of problem-solving by providing a structured approach to managing expressions involving powers.

The product of powers rule is a fundamental principle employed when multiplying expressions that share an identical base. This rule dictates that the exponents should be added together. Consider the expression $a^m \times a^n$; according to this rule, it simplifies to a^{m+n}. This process is particularly advantageous when dealing with multiple instances of the same variable or numerical base raised to various powers. For example, when faced with the expression $x^2 \times x^3$, applying the product of powers rule results in x^{2+3}, which further simplifies to x^5. This not only reduces the complexity of the expression but also facilitates quicker computations in subsequent steps.

The power of a power rule applies to situations where an already exponentiated term is raised to an additional power, as exemplified by the expression $(a^m)^n$. The simplification process involves multiplying the exponents together, yielding $a^{m \times n}$. For instance, when simplifying $(2^3)^2$, one multiplies the exponents 3 and 2, resulting in $2^{3 \times 2}$, or 2^6. This further simplifies to *64*, illustrating how the rule efficiently condenses the expression into a more manageable form.

The quotient of powers rule is utilized in scenarios where expressions with the same base are divided, necessitating the subtraction of the exponent in the denominator from the exponent in the numerator. The expression $a^m \div a^n$ thus simplifies to a^{m-n}. For example, when simplifying $x^5 \div x^2$, one subtracts the exponent 2 from 5, resulting in x^{5-2}, or x^3. This rule is crucial for reducing expressions to their simplest form, thereby facilitating easier manipulation in complex algebraic operations.

These exponent rules are not merely theoretical constructs but are actively applied in the realm of algebraic manipulations required for precise electrical calculations. For instance, when calculating electrical resistance in parallel circuits, the ability to simplify exponent terms is essential. By streamlining expressions through the application of these rules, one can achieve more efficient and accurate solutions, thereby enhancing the overall efficacy of the problem-solving process in electrical engineering contexts.

4.2: Roots and Their Uses

Square and Cube Numbers

Understanding the intricacies of square and cube numbers is critical for effectively addressing a variety of mathematical challenges, particularly those encountered on the IBEW aptitude test, which assesses mathematical reasoning and problem-solving skills. Square numbers, commonly referred to as perfect squares, are specific integers derived from the multiplication of an integer by itself, resulting in a product that represents the square of the original integer. For example, the integer *4* is classified as a square number because it is the result of multiplying *2* by itself, expressed mathematically as $2 \times 2 = 4$. Similarly, the integer exemplifies another square number, as it is the product of *3* multiplied by *3*, or $3 \times 3 = 9$. The ability to swiftly identify these numerical patterns is essential, as it can significantly reduce the time spent on calculations during the test.

In contrast, cube numbers are derived from a similar mathematical principle but involve an additional step: the integer is multiplied by itself twice more, effectively raising it to the third power. For instance, the number *8* qualifies as a cube number because it results from multiplying *2* by itself twice more, expressed as $2 \times 2 \times 2 = 8$. Likewise, *27* is recognized as the cube of *3*, as it results from the operation $3 \times 3 \times 3 = 27$.

To enhance proficiency in recognizing these numerical patterns, it is advantageous to commit to memory the first few square numbers, specifically *1, 4, 9, 16, 25, 36, 49, 64, 81, 100*, and cube numbers, such as *1, 8, 27, 64, 125*. This memorization can substantially augment one's ability to quickly identify these numbers in test questions, facilitating more efficient problem-solving. The utility of this knowledge extends beyond direct questions about squares and cubes; it also aids in the simplification of algebraic expressions and the resolution of equations. Recognizing a number as a square or cube can lead to more expedient solutions by simplifying the problem-solving process.

For example, consider the equation $x^2 = 49$. By identifying *49* as a square number, one can swiftly deduce that the possible values for *x* are *7* and *–7*, given that $7 \times 7 = 49$ and $(-7) \times (-7) = 49$. Similarly, in problems involving volume or three-dimensional geometry, recognizing that *64* is a cube number allows for the inference that an object with a volume of *64* cubic units must have side lengths measuring *4* units, since $4 \times 4 \times 4 = 64$.

Roots and Simplification

Roots and their simplification play a crucial role in mathematical operations, particularly when integrated with exponents, a fundamental concept for those preparing for the IBEW aptitude test. Achieving proficiency in decomposing radicals and skillfully integrating them with exponents optimizes problem-solving processes and enhances computational accuracy. This section delves into the intricate mechanics of simplifying square roots and cube roots, examining how these operations intersect with the established laws of exponents to enable more efficient resolution of algebraic expressions.

To simplify a radical, it is imperative to identify the factors of the radicand, which is the numerical value positioned beneath the radical sign, that are perfect squares or perfect cubes, contingent upon whether the operation involves a square root or a cube root. For instance, in the case of the square root of *48*, the factorization process reveals that *48* can be expressed as *16 × 3*, where *16* is recognized as a perfect square, being equivalent to 4^2. Consequently, the simplification of $\sqrt{48}$ proceeds as $\sqrt{16 \times 3} = 4\sqrt{3}$. This method effectively reduces the complexity of the radical, thereby facilitating its manipulation in algebraic equations.

When radicals are combined with exponents, the properties of exponents become integral to the simplification process. It is crucial to recall the exponentiation rule $(a^m)^n = a^{m \times n}$. This rule is particularly advantageous when simplifying expressions that involve roots raised to a power. For example, consider $(\sqrt{a})^2$, which translates to $a^{1/2 \times 2}$, illustrating how the operation of squaring a square root results in the original radicand. This property is indispensable for resolving equations where the variable is encapsulated within a radical.

Expressions that incorporate both roots and exponents necessitate the conversion of roots into fractional exponents. The expression $\sqrt[n]{a^m}$ is equivalent to $a^{m/n}$, a transformation that permits the application of exponent rules to streamline the expression. For instance, in the multiplication $a^{3/2} \times a^{1/2}$, the exponents are added according to the rule of exponent addition, resulting in $a^{(3/2)+(1/2)} = a^2$. This example underscores how a thorough comprehension of the interplay between roots and exponents can significantly simplify the process of combining and simplifying algebraic terms.

Chapter 5: Order of Operations (PEMDAS)

5.1: Applying the PEMDAS Rule

PEMDAS Sequence

The PEMDAS sequence is an essential concept within the field of mathematics, serving as the guiding principle for the systematic simplification of mathematical expressions and the accurate resolution of equations. This acronym denotes the specific order of operations: Parentheses, Exponents, Multiplication and Division (executed sequentially from left to right), and Addition and Subtraction (also executed sequentially from left to right). A comprehensive understanding and application of this sequence are vital for individuals preparing for the IBEW aptitude test, as it ensures the precise execution of mathematical operations in their intended order.

Commence by addressing any operations contained within **Parentheses**. For instance, consider the expression $3 \times (4 + 2)$. The initial step involves evaluating the sum within the parentheses: $4 + 2$, which yields 6. Subsequently, this result is multiplied by 3, resulting in a final value of 18. This step is critical because operations inside parentheses are prioritized to ensure accurate interpretation and calculation of the expression.

Proceed to the evaluation of **Exponents**, which include operations such as powers and roots, encompassing square roots, cube roots, and higher-order roots. In an expression like 2^3, the exponentiation must be calculated prior to any other operations, resulting in 8 (since 2 raised to the power of 3 equals $2 \times 2 \times 2$).

The subsequent phase involves **Multiplication and Division**, which hold equal precedence and are executed in the order they appear from left to right. For example, in the expression $8 \div 2 \times 4$, the division operation $8 \div 2$ is performed first, yielding 4. This intermediate result is then multiplied by 4, culminating in a product of 16.

Finally, address **Addition and Subtraction**, which are likewise of equal precedence and are executed from left to right. In the expression $10 - 2 + 4$, the subtraction $10 - 2$ is performed initially, resulting in 8. Subsequently, the addition of 4 to this result produces 12.

A common error encountered in mathematical calculations is the assumption that multiplication should always precede division or that addition should invariably precede subtraction. It is essential to emphasize that multiplication and division possess equal precedence, as do addition and subtraction. The correct methodology involves processing these operations sequentially from left to right as they appear in the expression.

Consider, for instance, the expression $4 + 18 \div 2^2 \times 3$. Adhering to the PEMDAS sequence, the first step is to resolve the exponent 2^2, resulting in 4. Subsequently, the division $18 \div 4$ is executed, yielding 4.5. Following this, the multiplication 4.5×3 is carried out, resulting in 13.5. Finally, the initial addition $4 + 13.5$ is performed, culminating in a final result of 17.5.

Complex Expressions

Handling complex expressions that contain nested parentheses necessitates meticulous adherence to the PEMDAS rule, which dictates the precise sequence in which operations must be executed to maintain mathematical accuracy. The PEMDAS acronym stands for Parentheses, Exponents, Multiplication and Division (from left to right), and Addition and Subtraction (from left to right). This sequence ensures that each operation is performed in the correct hierarchical order, with particular emphasis on resolving operations within parentheses first, starting from the innermost set and progressing outward.

Consider the expression $3 \times (4 + 2 \times (5 - 3)^2)$ for a detailed breakdown. The initial step involves identifying and simplifying the innermost parentheses, specifically $5 - 3$, which simplifies to 2. The next operation involves the exponentiation of this result, squaring 2 to yield 4. Consequently, the expression transforms into $3 \times (4 + 2 \times 4)$. At this juncture, focus shifts to the multiplication operation within the parentheses: 2×4, which results in 8. This intermediate result is then added to 4, producing 12. Finally, execute the multiplication of 3×12 to arrive at the final result of 36.

For expressions involving multiple layers of nested parentheses, such as $2 + (6 \times (4 + (3 - 1)^2))$, the process begins with the innermost parentheses: $3 - 1$, resulting in 2. Elevate this result by applying the exponent, squaring 2 to obtain 4. Substitute this value back into the expression, leading to $2 + (6 \times (4 + 4))$. The next step involves performing the addition within the parentheses, $4 + 4$, which simplifies to 8. Proceed with the multiplication 6×8, yielding 48. Finally, complete the expression by adding 2 to 48, culminating in 50.

When dealing with expressions that include variables and exponents, such as $5(2x + 3)^2 - 4x$, the approach requires an initial focus on simplifying the expression contained within the parentheses before applying any exponents. If the value of the variable x is provided, substitute it into the expression early in the process to streamline calculations. In instances where the variable's value is not specified, proceed with symbolic manipulation to simplify the expression as thoroughly as possible, ensuring that each step adheres to the PEMDAS order of operations to prevent computational errors.

5.2: Practice and Pitfalls

Avoiding Mistakes

One of the most prevalent mistakes when applying the PEMDAS rule is the incorrect execution of the prescribed sequence of operations, particularly during the stages involving multiplication and division, or addition and subtraction. Within these operation pairs, it is crucial to adhere to the left-to-right execution order, which explicitly dictates that multiplication does not inherently take precedence over division, nor does addition automatically precede subtraction. For instance, consider the expression $12 \div 3 \times 2$. The correct approach involves executing the division operation first, dividing 12 by 3, resulting in a quotient of 4. Subsequently, the result of this division is multiplied by 2, yielding a final product of 8. This sequence should be meticulously followed to ensure accurate results.

Another frequent error stems from a misinterpretation of the hierarchical structure of operations, particularly when parentheses are present within an expression. A common oversight is the premature simplification of elements external to the parentheses before thoroughly resolving the expressions contained within them. For example, in the expression $2 + 3 \times (4 + 2)$, the correct protocol involves initially addressing the operation inside the parentheses: adding 4 and 2 to obtain 6. Following this, the result 6 is multiplied by 3, producing 18. Finally, the addition of 2 results in 20. Any attempt to multiply 3×4 prior to resolving the parentheses will lead to an erroneous outcome.

Misapplication of the rules governing exponents can also result in significant errors. Exponents must be addressed immediately after any operations within parentheses, but prior to engaging in any multiplication, division, addition, or subtraction. Neglecting this order can drastically affect the final result. For instance, in the expression $2^3 \times 4$, the exponentiation is performed first, whereby 2^3 is calculated as 8. This result is then multiplied by 4, yielding a final product of 32. Disregarding the rule for exponents and prematurely multiplying 2 by 4 before applying the exponent would lead to an incorrect calculation.

To mitigate these errors, it is advisable to engage in practice with a diverse range of expressions, progressively increasing in complexity, while meticulously applying each step of the PEMDAS rule. Additionally, double-checking calculations by systematically revisiting each step can serve as a safeguard against mistakes. Articulating the rationale behind each procedural step, whether verbally or in written form, can further reinforce the correct application of the order of operations, ensuring a robust understanding and execution of the PEMDAS rule.

Timed Drills for Speed and Confidence

Timed drills constitute an integral component in the acquisition of proficiency in the Order of Operations, a fundamental competency for individuals preparing for the International Brotherhood of Electrical Workers (IBEW) aptitude test. The primary objective of these drills is to enhance both the speed and accuracy with which candidates can solve mathematical problems, thereby enabling them to navigate the exam's stringent time limitations effectively. Achieving success in this endeavor is contingent upon engaging in regular, concentrated practice sessions that replicate the conditions of the actual test environment as closely as possible.

Commence by allocating a fixed period each day exclusively for practice, thereby establishing a routine that fosters consistency. Employ a timing device to instill a sense of urgency, initially setting a lenient time constraint for each individual problem. As the individual's proficiency in solving these problems increases, incrementally reduce the allotted time. This methodology facilitates acclimatization to exam conditions, ensuring that candidates maintain accuracy in their calculations while under pressure.

Initiate the practice regimen with elementary expressions that adhere to the PEMDAS rule, such as *3 + 4 % 2* or *$5^2 - 9$*. These preliminary drills are designed to reinforce the correct hierarchical sequence of operations: Parentheses, Exponents, Multiplication and Division (executed from left to right), followed by Addition and Subtraction (also executed from left to right). As the candidate's confidence builds, progress to more intricate problems that involve multiple operational steps and nested parentheses, exemplified by expressions like $2 + (3 \times (2^2 - 1))$.

Construct a varied collection of problems that span a spectrum of difficulty levels and complexities to ensure comprehensive practice. This approach mitigates the risk of developing predictable problem-solving patterns, thereby equipping candidates to tackle the diverse and unpredictable nature of potential test questions. Upon completion of each drill, conduct a thorough analysis of the solutions to identify any deviations from the correct sequence of operations or calculation errors. This meticulous review process is critical for assimilating knowledge from mistakes and preventing their recurrence in subsequent practice sessions.

Participate in peer review sessions whenever feasible. Articulating your reasoning and solution methodology to another individual solidifies your comprehension and can expose any deficiencies in your understanding. Utilize the array of online resources and practice tests available specifically for the IBEW aptitude test, directing your focus toward sections that present challenges to your mastery of the Order of Operations.

As the examination date approaches, amplify both the frequency and intensity of the timed drills. Recreate the test environment by practicing in a serene, distraction-free setting, employing only the materials permissible during the actual exam. This rigorous level of preparation not only fortifies the requisite mathematical skills but also cultivates the mental stamina necessary to effectively manage the pressures inherent in the testing environment.

Chapter 6: Percents, Ratios & Proportions

6.1: Percent Concepts and Calculations

Understanding Percents

Percents, a fundamental concept in mathematics, represent parts of a whole as fractions of 100, a crucial representation that finds extensive application across various domains. This concept is indispensable in fields such as finance, where it is used to calculate interest rates, returns on investment, and profit margins, as well as in data analysis for determining growth rates, statistical deviations, and percentage distributions. It is also essential for solving problems related to percentage increase, percentage decrease, and discount calculations, which are frequently encountered in the IBEW aptitude test. Aspiring electricians and apprentices must develop a thorough understanding of how to manipulate percents, as this skill directly translates to practical tasks such as calculating voltage drops in electrical circuits, determining resistance increases due to temperature changes or material properties, and computing discounts on electrical materials and components.

When addressing increase and decrease problems, a comprehensive understanding of the basic formula for percent change is required: $\frac{new\ value - original\ value}{original\ value} \times 100$. This formula is essential for quantifying the extent to which a particular quantity has increased or decreased in terms of percentage. To illustrate, consider a scenario where the resistance of a copper wire increases from 10 ohms to 15 ohms due to a rise in temperature. The percent increase in resistance is computed as $\frac{15-10}{10} \times 100\% = 50\%$, signifying a 50% increase in resistance, which could impact the performance of an electrical circuit by altering current flow and potentially causing overheating.

In solving discount problems, it is necessary to accurately calculate the reduction on a price, a critical skill for effectively managing project budgets and ensuring cost efficiency. The formula used to determine the discount amount is $discount = original\ price \times \frac{discount\ rate}{100}$. For instance, if an electrical component originally priced at $200 is available at a 10% discount, the discount amount is calculated as 200 \times \frac{{10}}{{100}} = $20. This results in a reduced sale price of $200 - $20 = $180, which can significantly affect the overall cost of a project, especially when purchasing in bulk.

Understanding the effective rate becomes crucial when dealing with multiple percentage changes applied in succession, as this reflects the non-linear nature of percentage operations. For example, if the price of a piece of equipment initially increases by 10% and subsequently decreases by 10%, the net effect is not a return to the original price. This is due to the non-commutative property of percentage operations, where the order of applying percentage changes affects the final outcome. Calculating the final price involves applying each percentage change sequentially, demonstrating that the final price is not simply the original price but rather a product of the compounded effects of each percentage change.

To achieve mastery of these concepts, one must engage with practical, real-world scenarios, such as calculating the total cost of electrical materials after applying a series of discounts or determining the final resistance of a circuit after accounting for a percentage increase due to thermal expansion or other factors. Consistent practice with these types of problems will build proficiency and ensure preparedness for the IBEW aptitude test, equipping aspiring electricians with the necessary skills to excel in their field.

Conversions: Percent, Decimal, Fraction

Mastering the precise techniques for converting between percents, decimals, and fractions is essential for success on the IBEW aptitude test and has significant implications for practical applications within the electrical field. This competency is crucial for ensuring the accuracy of calculations related to electrical measurements, financial budgeting, and meticulous project planning.

To convert a percentage to a decimal, one must divide by 100, effectively shifting the decimal point two positions to the left. For example, transforming *25%* into a decimal involves dividing the numeral *25* by *100*, resulting in *0.25*. This conversion process is indispensable when conducting calculations that involve voltage drop assessments or quantifying increases in electrical resistance, where precise decimal values are essential for accurate computation.

When converting a decimal into a percentage, the operation entails multiplying the decimal by 100, moving the decimal point two positions to the right. For instance, converting *0.75* into a percentage requires multiplying *0.75* by *100*, yielding *75%*. This conversion is particularly beneficial when evaluating the efficiency of electrical components or calculating the percentage of power loss during electrical transmission, as expressing values as percentages provides clearer insights into performance metrics.

Converting a fraction into a decimal necessitates dividing the numerator by the denominator.

For example, the fraction $\frac{1}{4}$ is converted into *0.25* by dividing *1* by *4*. This skill is vital for interpreting numerical values in electrical schematics, where decimal representations facilitate the understanding of precise measurements and ensure accuracy in material estimations and resource allocation.

To transform a decimal into a fraction, one must determine the place value of the decimal, using this place value as the denominator, and simplifying the fraction if necessary. For instance, converting the decimal *0.5* into a fraction involves recognizing that the digit *5* occupies the tenths place, thus forming the fraction $\frac{5}{10}$, which simplifies to $\frac{1}{2}$. This conversion is essential for comprehending ratios in wiring diagrams or performing load calculations, where fractional representations clarify proportional relationships.

When converting a percentage directly into a fraction, the percentage value is positioned over *100* and then simplified. For example, *50%* is transformed into the fraction $\frac{50}{100}$, which simplifies to $\frac{1}{2}$. This method is critical for calculating the proportions of components within an electrical circuit or determining the distribution of loads across various sections of an electrical system, where precise fractional values are necessary for maintaining balance and efficiency.

6.2: Ratios and Proportions

Ratios and Rates

Understanding the intricacies of ratios and rates is crucial for individuals preparing for the IBEW aptitude test, as these mathematical constructs are fundamental to both theoretical and practical applications in the field of electrical work. A ratio serves as a quantitative comparison between two distinct quantities, illustrating the relative magnitude of one quantity in relation to the other. This is typically denoted in the form $a : b$ or a/b, where a and b represent the quantities being compared. In contrast, a rate is a specialized form of ratio that contrasts two quantities with differing units of measurement, such as miles per hour (*mph*) or watts per hour (W/h), thereby providing a measure of how one quantity changes in relation to another over a specified unit of time or space.

The meticulous application of units in calculations is paramount to ensure that comparisons are not only accurate but also applicable to real-world scenarios. For instance, when calculating the speed at which electrical current flows, one might employ the rate $amps/hour(A/h)$. This specific rate quantifies the number of amperes of electrical current that traverse a given point within an hour, which is critical for evaluating both the efficiency and safety of electrical systems. Accurate application of this rate facilitates precise assessments of system performance, ensuring that electrical installations operate within safe and efficient parameters.

Consider an illustrative example that highlights the use of ratios and rates in electrical applications:

Suppose a circuit requires a current of *10A* to operate optimally, and you possess a power source with a capacity to supply *40A*. The ratio of the power source's capacity to the circuit's demand is expressed as *40:10*, which simplifies to *4:1*. This simplified ratio reveals that the power source can supply four times the current necessary for the circuit's operation. Such a ratio indicates potential for increased efficiency or, conversely, the need for system modifications to prevent the risk of overload, which could lead to equipment damage or safety hazards.

When examining rates, consider the evaluation of an appliance's energy consumption over a given period. If an appliance consumes *300W* over a duration of *2* hours, the consumption rate is calculated as $150W/h$. This rate is instrumental in determining the cost of energy usage and assessing the appliance's efficiency. Understanding and applying this rate is vital for both practical electrical work and the theoretical knowledge required for success on the IBEW aptitude test, as it provides insights into energy management and cost optimization.

To ensure that units are applied with precision and relevance, it is essential to adhere to a systematic process:

1. **Identify** the specific units involved in your calculation, ensuring clarity in the measurement and comparison of quantities.

2. **Convert** units when necessary to align with the context of the problem, such as converting kilowatts (*kW*) to watts (*W*) for calculations involving smaller scale systems, thereby maintaining consistency and accuracy in the analysis.

3. **Apply** the ratio or rate to solve the problem at hand, ensuring that your solution is pertinent to the scenario and accurately reflects the underlying physical principles at play. This thorough approach guarantees that the results are both meaningful and applicable to the practical challenges encountered in electrical work.

Solving Proportions with Cross-Multiplication

Cross-multiplication provides a systematic approach to solving equations involving proportions, a technique that proves essential in the field of electrical engineering for tasks such as calculating precise current flows or determining the appropriate resistor values required to achieve specific electrical characteristics. A proportion is defined when two ratios are equivalent, typically expressed in the format $a : b = c : d$, where a, b, c, and d represent the individual terms of the ratio. This method becomes particularly advantageous when one of these terms is unknown and must be calculated.

The procedure of cross-multiplication involves multiplying the terms that are diagonally opposite each other, referred to as the outer terms, and setting this product equal to the product of the inner terms. This operation results in an equation that can be manipulated algebraically to solve for the unknown variable. For instance, given the proportion expressed as $\frac{a}{b} = \frac{c}{d}$, applying cross-multiplication yields the equation $ad = bc$. In scenarios where one of the terms is unknown, the equation can be rearranged to isolate and solve for the unknown term, providing a clear path to the solution.

Consider a practical application in electrical engineering: determining the necessary resistance in a circuit to achieve a desired voltage drop V at a specific current I, given known values from a similar circuit configuration. Suppose the known voltage and current values are $V_1 = 10V$ and $I_1 = 2A$, respectively, and the task is to find the voltage V_2 when the current changes to $I_2 = 4A$. By establishing the proportion $V_1 / I_1 = V_2 / I_2$ and employing cross-multiplication, we have $10V / 2A = V_2 / 4A$. This simplifies to the equation $20V = 2A \cdot V_2$. Solving for V_2, we find that $V_2 = 10V$, indicating that the voltage drop remains consistent despite changes in current. This constancy is critical in designing and troubleshooting electrical systems, as it ensures stability and predictability in circuit behavior.

Beyond direct electrical calculations, the utility of cross-multiplication extends into areas such as financial management, including budgeting and cost estimation, where proportional relationships are frequently encountered. Mastery of this technique enhances analytical and problem-solving skills, equipping aspiring electricians with the ability to address a diverse array of challenges encountered both in professional practice and during assessments such as the IBEW aptitude test.

Word Problems: Percent and Ratio Skills

To effectively address word problems involving percents and ratios, it is imperative to employ a structured methodology that translates the given textual information into precise mathematical expressions. These problems frequently replicate real-world scenarios, making them especially pertinent for individuals aiming to excel in the IBEW aptitude test for electricians. A thorough comprehension of the fundamental principles governing percents and ratios, coupled with the ability to apply these principles with confidence, is indispensable.

When faced with a problem involving percents, the initial step involves accurately identifying the base or whole quantity to which the percent is applicable. This base serves as the reference point since the percent signifies a fraction of this base. For instance, in a situation where a circuit's efficiency is enhanced by *25%* following modifications from an initial efficiency of *80%*, the task is to compute the new efficiency level. This involves calculating *25%* of the initial *80%*, which is mathematically represented as *0.25 × 80 = 20%*. By adding this calculated percentage increase to the original *80%*, the circuit's updated efficiency is determined to be *100%*.

Ratios, which serve as a comparative tool between two quantities, are directly applicable to various electrical concepts such as resistance ratios in circuits or the ratio of voltage to current. When addressing ratio problems, it is crucial to ensure that the units used in the comparison remain consistent throughout the process. For example, consider a scenario where one wire conducts a current of *2A* while another wire conducts *4A*. The ratio of their currents is initially expressed as *2 : 4*, which can be simplified to *1 : 2* by dividing both terms by their greatest common divisor. This simplification effectively clarifies the proportional relationship without altering the fundamental nature of the comparison.

A typical application of ratios in the realm of electrical work involves determining the necessary length of wire for specific installations. Imagine a project that necessitates a wire length that is double the distance between two points, which measures *15* feet. To solve this, establish the problem as a ratio of *1 : 2* (distance to wire length), where the variable x represents the required wire length. By setting up the proportion $15/x = 1/2$ and employing cross-multiplication, the equation *2 × 15 = x* is derived, yielding a solution of *x = 30* feet for the necessary wire length.

To refine problem-solving capabilities, it is beneficial to practice with a wide range of scenarios, progressively increasing in complexity. Start with fundamental percent increases or decreases and straightforward ratios, then advance to more intricate multi-step problems that integrate both percents and ratios. Utilize a methodical, step-by-step approach to dissect the problem, translate the verbal description into mathematical expressions, and solve, all while ensuring logical consistency in the final answer to foster confidence.

Chapter 7: Word Problem Strategies

7.1: Solving Word Problems Effectively

Translating to Math

Translating real-world phrases into solvable equations is an essential skill for effectively navigating the IBEW aptitude test and achieving proficiency in the electrical field. This intricate process necessitates the precise identification of mathematical operations as described in the problem text and their accurate representation through algebraic expressions, ensuring that each component of the problem is thoroughly understood and correctly translated.

The initial step involves a meticulous examination to identify the specific quantities involved in the problem, such as distances measured in meters or kilometers, costs expressed in dollars or other currencies, times given in seconds, minutes, or hours, or electrical measurements like voltage in volts or current in amperes. For instance, consider a word problem that states, "A circuit carries a current of 3 amps and needs to be split into three equal parts." In this scenario, the relevant quantities include the total current, which is 3 amperes, and the number of parts, which is 3, indicating the need for division.

Subsequently, it is crucial to determine the exact mathematical operations required by the problem, which may include addition, subtraction, multiplication, division, or comparisons such as greater than or less than. In our example, the operation needed is division, as we aim to split the current equally among the parts, necessitating the division of the total current by the number of parts.

The next step involves translating the word problem into a precise equation. For the current example, if   denotes the current in each individual part of the circuit, the equation becomes $3 \div 3 = I$, which simplifies to $I = 1$. This indicates that each segment of the circuit carries a current of 1 amp, achieving the desired division.

Consider a different example: "If a resistor decreases the current in a circuit by 2 amps every 5 seconds, how much will the current decrease in 20 seconds?" In this case, the quantities are the rate of decrease, which is 2 amps per 5 seconds, and the total time, which is 20 seconds. The required operation is multiplication, as we need to calculate the cumulative decrease over the specified time period. The equation is formulated as $(2\,amps/5\,seconds) \times 20\,seconds = \Delta I$, where ΔI represents the change in current. Simplifying this yields $\Delta I = 8$ amps, indicating a total decrease of 8 amps over the 20-second duration.

To refine your problem-solving skills, it is beneficial to engage in practice with a wide array of scenarios, thereby developing fluency in identifying the mathematical operations implied by the text. It is advisable to systematically write down known quantities and the unknowns to be determined, as this approach aids in structuring the equation logically. Utilizing units as a guide in setting up equations can help ensure accuracy, as matching units on both sides of the equation can serve as a verification tool. Solving problems step-by-step is particularly important, especially for complex problems that involve multiple operations or sequential steps, as this methodical approach minimizes errors and enhances clarity.

Spotting Clues

Identifying and interpreting clues embedded within word problems is an essential competency for test-takers aiming to unravel the mathematical operations necessary to derive a solution. This competency hinges on the precise recognition of specific keywords and phrases that serve as indicators for the requisite computational actions. For example, the presence of terms such as "total," "sum," or "combined" directly signals the operation of addition, suggesting that quantities are to be aggregated. Conversely, the term "difference" unequivocally points towards subtraction, indicating the need to calculate the disparity between quantities. The ability to discern these indicators facilitates the methodical decomposition of the problem into a mathematical equation that is amenable to resolution.

To proficiently identify these clues, one should begin by meticulously reading the problem statement, ensuring a comprehensive understanding of the context and the question being posed. During this process, it is beneficial to underline or highlight keywords that denote specific mathematical operations. For instance, the phrase "per unit" often suggests that a division operation is necessary to ascertain the cost or value of a single item when provided with the total cost for a collection of items. In a similar vein, the phrase "times as much" typically signals multiplication, particularly in scenarios involving comparative analysis or proportional relationships.

Upon the identification of operational keywords, the subsequent step involves constructing a systematic solution strategy. This begins with the definition of the unknown variable, which represents the quantity or value that the problem seeks to determine. Assigning a symbol, such as x, to this unknown variable aids in the formulation of an algebraic expression or equation that encapsulates the problem's essence. For instance, consider a scenario where a problem states, "a wire is three times as long as another wire," and the length of the shorter wire is known. In this case, the length of the longer wire can be represented algebraically as $3x$, where x denotes the length of the shorter wire.

The translation of the word problem into a mathematical model involves inserting the identified numerical values and operations into an equation informed by the detected clues. In cases where the problem necessitates sequential operations or the application of multiple operations, adherence to the order of operations—PEMDAS (Parentheses, Exponents, Multiplication and Division, Addition and Subtraction)—is crucial to maintain computational accuracy.

Consider a practical example: a problem might inquire about the number of circuits that can be constructed using a given length of wire, with each circuit requiring a specified length. Suppose you have *60* feet of wire, and each circuit necessitates *15* feet. The clue "each," which implies division, leads to the formation of the equation $60 \div 15 = x$. Solving this equation yields $x = 4$, indicating that it is possible to construct four circuits with the available wire.

Common Word Problem Types

Mastering the intricacies of common word problem types, including rate, distance, mixture, and work scenarios, is essential for achieving proficiency on the IBEW aptitude test. These problems effectively integrate real-world applications with mathematical principles, offering a comprehensive framework for interpreting abstract concepts through practical means. We will meticulously analyze each type, concentrating on the mathematical techniques required to solve them with precision.

Rate problems encompass situations where an object or individual maintains a uniform speed, necessitating the determination of either the speed, the distance traversed, or the time elapsed. The core formula employed is *Distance = Rate × Time* or *D = RT*. For instance, consider an electrician traveling at a constant velocity of 60 miles per hour over a duration of 2 hours. The calculation of the distance covered involves multiplying the rate by the time, yielding *60 × 2 = 120* miles. The initial step involves identifying the known quantities and the variable that requires solving. Subsequently, manipulate the equation by isolating the unknown variable to resolve the problem effectively.

Distance problems emphasize the spatial dimension, such as determining the length of wire necessary to connect two distinct points. It is advantageous to construct a visual representation of the problem, often in the form of a diagram, to facilitate comprehension. Suppose two points are separated by a distance of 100 feet, and the task involves installing a wire with an additional 10% allowance for slack. The calculation for the total wire length required is *100 + (0.10 × 100) = 110* feet. A thorough understanding of proportions and the concept of scaling is crucial for accurately solving these problems.

Mixture problems entail the combination of substances in specific ratios to achieve a desired composition. This involves setting up equations based on the quantities and concentrations of the individual components. For instance, if tasked with creating 100 gallons of a 40% concentration solution by combining two solutions with concentrations of 30% and 50%, one can employ the method of weighted averages or establish a system of linear equations. These equations will enable the calculation of the precise volumes of each solution required to achieve the target concentration.

Work problems are concerned with determining the time required for individuals or machines to complete a task based on their respective rates of work. The formula *Work = Rate × Time* is applicable here, with work typically represented as a fraction of task completion. Consider a scenario where one machine completes a task in 5 hours, while another accomplishes it in 3 hours. To find the combined rate of work, sum their individual rates: $\frac{1}{5}+\frac{1}{3}$. To add these fractions, convert them to a common denominator, resulting in $\frac{3}{15}+\frac{5}{15}=\frac{8}{15}$ of the task per hour.

Mastery of fraction addition and manipulation is an invaluable strategy in addressing these types of problems.

Practice Sets and Solutions

To effectively prepare for the IBEW aptitude test, it is crucial to engage with practice sets that are meticulously designed to mirror the conditions and challenges of the actual test environment. These practice sets are invaluable, as they not only reinforce problem-solving strategies but also provide hands-on experience in tackling word problems, which represent a significant component of the exam. Let us delve into a practice set that applies these strategies specifically to word problems, with an emphasis on translating real-world scenarios into solvable mathematical equations and identifying the clues that dictate the necessary mathematical operations.

Practice Problem 1:
Consider a scenario where an electrician is tasked with installing a series of lights along a pathway that stretches for a total length of 120 feet. The requirement is to place each light at an interval of 15 feet, ensuring that there is a light positioned both at the start and at the end of the path. The question is to determine the total number of lights required for the installation.

Solution:
To approach this problem, it is essential to recognize that it involves a linear sequence where there is uniform spacing between each light fixture. The total length of the path is specified as 120 feet, while the interval between consecutive lights is 15 feet. The first step is to calculate the number of intervals between the lights by dividing the total path length by the spacing distance: $120 \div 15 = 8$. This calculation yields the number of spaces between the lights. However, since a light is required at both the beginning and the end of the path, it is necessary to add one additional light to account for the starting point. Therefore, the total number of lights needed is $8 + 1 = 9$.

Practice Problem 2:
In this problem, a circuit is described that includes a resistor which causes a voltage drop of 5 volts for every 2 amperes of current that flows through it. The task is to determine the total voltage drop across the resistor when the current is increased to 8 amperes.

Solution:
This scenario involves a direct proportional relationship between the current flowing through the resistor and the resulting voltage drop. Initially, the ratio of voltage drop to current is given

as *5V : 2A*. With the current increasing to 8 amperes, it is necessary to set up a proportion to calculate the new voltage drop, denoted as: $V : \dfrac{5V}{2A} = \dfrac{V}{8A}$. To solve for V, cross-multiply to obtain the equation $2A \cdot V = 5V \cdot 8A$. Simplifying this equation results in . Consequently, the total voltage drop across the resistor when the current is 8 amperes is 20 volts.

Practice Problem 3:
An apprentice electrician is capable of completing a specific wiring task independently in 6 hours, while a journeyman electrician can accomplish the same task in 4 hours. The problem is to determine the time it would take for both electricians to complete the task if they work together.

Solution:
To solve this problem, it is necessary to calculate the combined rate of work when both electricians are working simultaneously. This is done by adding the reciprocals of their individual times to complete the task. The apprentice's rate of work is $\dfrac{1}{6}$ of the task per hour, and the journeyman's rate is $\dfrac{1}{4}$ of the task per hour. To add these rates, find a common denominator, which is 12, resulting in $\dfrac{2}{12} + \dfrac{3}{12} = \dfrac{5}{12}$. The combined rate of work is $\dfrac{5}{12}$ of the task per hour. To find the total time taken when they work together, take the reciprocal of the combined rate, yielding $\dfrac{12}{5}$ hours, which simplifies to 2.4 hours. Thus, working together, the apprentice and journeyman can complete the task in 2.4 hours.

Chapter 8: Algebra Basics

8.1: Core Concepts

What Is Algebra?

Algebra is an essential component in the field of mathematics, particularly for individuals pursuing a career in the electrical sector and striving to excel in the International Brotherhood of Electrical Workers (IBEW) aptitude test. This branch of mathematics focuses on the manipulation of symbolic representations, categorized as variables and constants, to effectively solve equations and understand the intricate relationships between different quantities. Variables, typically denoted by letters such as *x* or *y*, serve as placeholders for values that are currently unknown or may vary within a given context. In contrast, constants are specific numerical values that remain unchanged throughout the course of an equation, exemplified by numbers like *2*, *5*, or the mathematical constant π.

The application of algebra in problem-solving within the electrical domain is both profound and multifaceted. It enables practitioners to abstract and extrapolate from individual cases to broader principles, a process that is critical when diagnosing issues within electrical circuits, calculating electrical loads with precision, and optimizing the layout of wiring systems for efficiency. A prime example of algebra's utility is Ohm's Law, a fundamental concept in electrical engineering, articulated in algebraic form as *V=IR*. In this equation, signifies the voltage across a component, *I* represents the current flowing through it, and *R* denotes the resistance it presents. This equation highlights the interrelated nature of voltage, current, and resistance, providing electricians with the ability to calculate any one of these variables, given the other two are known.

Proficiency in algebra significantly enhances an individual's ability to comprehend and solve linear equations, systems of equations, and quadratic equations, all of which are pivotal for modeling and addressing practical electrical challenges. For instance, determining the total resistance in a parallel circuit necessitates solving a system of equations, with each equation delineating a distinct path for the flow of current. This requires the application of the formula for total resistance in parallel circuits, $\frac{1}{R_{total}} = \frac{1}{R_1} + \frac{1}{R_2} + ... + \frac{1}{R_n}$, where each *R* represents the resistance of an individual pathway.

Mastery of algebraic concepts is crucial for individuals preparing for the IBEW aptitude test. It equips test-takers with the confidence needed to confront mathematical problems, employing logical reasoning to adeptly manipulate equations and isolate variables with precision. This skill set is indispensable for fostering a successful career in the electrical trade, where the ability to solve complex problems and engage in analytical thinking is of paramount importance.

Expressions vs. Equations

Understanding the distinction between algebraic expressions and equations is a fundamental aspect of algebra that underpins effective problem-solving. An algebraic expression is a mathematical phrase that combines numbers, variables, and operational symbols, such as addition (+), subtraction (−), multiplication (×), and division (□), to denote a particular numerical value or set of values. Unlike an equation, an expression does not incorporate an equality sign (=) and thus does not assert the equality between two distinct quantities. For instance, consider the expression $3x + 5$; it is a linear expression comprising a variable x multiplied by a coefficient 3, with a constant term 5 added. Similarly, $2y^2 - 4$ is a quadratic expression where the variable y is squared, multiplied by the coefficient 2, and subtracted by the constant 4. Both examples illustrate expressions whose values are contingent on the specific values assigned to their respective variables, x and y.

Conversely, an equation is a formal statement that affirms the equivalence of two expressions by employing an equality sign (=). This mathematical construct establishes a relationship between two expressions, typically involving one or more variables, and posits that the expressions on either side of the equality sign yield identical values under certain conditions. For example, the equation $3x + 5 = 11$ posits that the sum of three times a variable x and the constant 5 is equal to 11. The primary task when engaging with equations is to ascertain the specific value or values of the variable(s) that render the equation true, thereby satisfying the equation's condition of equality.

A comprehensive understanding of algebraic principles is imperative for the proficient manipulation of expressions and equations. Simplifying an expression involves systematically combining like terms—terms that contain the same variables raised to identical powers—and applying the distributive property where necessary. For instance, in the expression $2x + 3x - 5$, the terms $2x$ and $3x$ are like terms, both involving the variable x raised to the first power. By combining these terms, one simplifies the expression to $5x - 5$, achieving a more concise representation without altering the expression's inherent value.

Solving equations entails determining the variable's value that satisfies the equation, typically by isolating the variable on one side of the equation. Consider the equation $3x + 5 = 11$; to solve for x, one must first eliminate the constant term on the left side by subtracting 5 from both sides, resulting in the simplified equation $3x = 6$. Subsequently, dividing both sides by the coefficient 3 isolates the variable, yielding $x = 2$. This solution indicates that substituting $x = 2$ into the original equation satisfies the equality, thereby confirming the solution's validity.

A critical competency in managing both expressions and equations is the adeptness in reversing operations. When solving equations, it is essential to systematically undo operations applied to the variable to achieve isolation. This process necessitates a thorough comprehension of the properties of equality, such as the addition and multiplication properties, alongside a meticulous adherence to the order of operations, commonly known as PEMDAS (Parentheses, Exponents, Multiplication and Division, Addition and Subtraction). Ensuring each operational step is logically sequenced and mathematically sound is paramount in achieving accurate and reliable solutions.

Using Variables in Context

In the specialized domain of electrical engineering, algebra serves as an essential analytical tool, enabling professionals to translate complex real-world electrical problems into solvable mathematical equations. This process involves the use of variables, which are symbols that represent unknown or variable quantities, allowing for the formulation of algebraic expressions that can be systematically manipulated to obtain solutions. Mastery of this skill is indispensable for those aspiring to excel in the electrical field, particularly for candidates preparing for the IBEW aptitude test, where proficiency in algebraic reasoning is crucial.

Consider a scenario where an electrician must calculate the total current (I) flowing through a circuit, given the circuit's voltage (V) and resistance (R). The application of Ohm's Law, articulated as $V = IR$, provides a direct computational approach. For a circuit with a voltage of *120* volts and a resistance of *30* ohms, one must rearrange the equation to solve for the current. Substituting the known values into the equation yields *120* = *I* x *30*. To isolate *I*, divide both sides of the equation by *30*, resulting in $I = \dfrac{120}{30}$, which simplifies to *I* = *4* amps. In this context, the variables *V*, *I*, and *R* are not mere symbols but represent specific physical quantities within the electrical framework, illustrating the seamless integration of abstract algebraic concepts with concrete electrical realities.

In another instance, electricians frequently need to compute the power (P) dissipated by an electrical device, utilizing the power formula $P = IV$, where *I* denotes the current flowing through the device and *V* represents the voltage across it. For a device that draws a current of *2* amps while operating at a voltage of *120* volts, the power calculation becomes a straightforward multiplication: *P* = *2* x *120*. This operation results in a power dissipation of *240* watts. This example underscores the practicality of algebra in facilitating rapid and precise calculations that are vital for the proper installation and effective troubleshooting of electrical systems.

Furthermore, algebra is instrumental in calculating the total resistance (R_{total}) of resistors arranged in parallel. The formula $\dfrac{1}{R_{total}} = \dfrac{1}{R_1} + \dfrac{1}{R_2} + ... + \dfrac{1}{R_n}$ embodies fundamental algebraic principles. To determine the total resistance for two resistors with resistances of *4* ohms and *6* ohms, the equation becomes $\dfrac{1}{R_{total}} = \dfrac{1}{4} + \dfrac{1}{6}$. Converting the fractions to a common denominator, the equation simplifies to $\dfrac{1}{R_{total}} = \dfrac{3}{12} + \dfrac{2}{12} = \dfrac{5}{12}$. Solving for R_{total} involves taking the reciprocal of $\dfrac{5}{12}$, resulting in $R_{total} \dfrac{12}{5}$, or *2.4* ohms. This calculation exemplifies the application of algebraic

methods to derive precise electrical parameters, essential for designing and analyzing complex electrical circuits.

8.2: Language and Structure

Algebra Vocabulary

In the realm of algebra, a profound comprehension of the specific terminology is as crucial as mastering the operational techniques. The elements known as terms, coefficients, and operators constitute the fundamental building blocks that construct algebraic expressions and equations, serving as the essential groundwork for more sophisticated algebraic concepts.

A term in algebra is defined as a singular mathematical entity, which can manifest as a standalone number, an isolated variable, or a composite product of numbers and variables interconnected through multiplication or division. Consider the algebraic expression $7x^2 - 3xy + 5$; within this expression, there exist three distinct terms: $7x^2$, $-3xy$, and *5*. Each term distinctly contributes to the overall value of the expression, with $7x^2$ representing a quadratic term where the variable x is squared and multiplied by *7*, $-3xy$ denoting a product of two variables x and y with a negative coefficient, and *5* being a constant term.

The coefficient specifically refers to the numeric factor that multiplies a variable within a term, thereby quantifying the variable's influence in that term. In the term $7x^2$, the numeral *7* functions as the coefficient, signifying that the squared variable $x2$ is multiplied by the value of *7*. Coefficients can possess positive or negative values, and they may be expressed as whole numbers or fractions, such as $\dfrac{3}{4}$ or -2. A thorough understanding of coefficients is imperative for the manipulation of algebraic expressions, particularly in the processes of simplification or equation resolution, as coefficients dictate the magnitude of each variable's impact.

Operators are the symbolic representations of mathematical operations. The four fundamental operators consist of addition (+), subtraction (−), multiplication (×), and division (□). In algebraic contexts, operators serve as the connectors between terms, forming complete expressions or equations. For instance, the addition operator in the expression $x + 5$ indicates the operation of adding the constant *5* to the variable x. Mastery in recognizing and applying operators is crucial for the resolution of algebraic problems, as the correct interpretation of these symbols determines the sequence and nature of the operations performed.

The precise identification of these components is vital when engaging with algebraic expressions. To simplify the expression $2x + 3x$, it is essential to recognize that the numbers 2 and 3 function as the coefficients of the variable x, and the operation indicated by the operator $+$ involves addition. By combining these like terms, the expression is simplified to $5x$, demonstrating the direct influence that coefficients and operators exert in the process of simplification. This example illustrates the necessity of understanding how coefficients dictate the aggregation of terms and how operators guide the operational procedures within algebraic expressions.

Order of Operations in Algebra

Understanding and applying the Order of Operations, commonly abbreviated as PEMDAS, is essential for the precise simplification of algebraic expressions and the accurate resolution of equations. PEMDAS delineates the specific sequence in which mathematical operations must be performed to ensure uniformity and precision in results across diverse mathematical challenges. The acronym PEMDAS stands for Parentheses, Exponents, Multiplication and Division (executed from left to right), and Addition and Subtraction (also executed from left to right).

Consider the algebraic expression $3 + 4 \times 2^2$. In the absence of an internationally recognized order of operations, simplifying this expression might yield multiple interpretations and results. However, by adhering to PEMDAS, we can methodically solve this problem. The procedure begins with addressing Exponents, where 2^2 is calculated as 4. The next step involves handling Multiplication, where 4×4 yields 16. The final operation involves Addition, where $3 + 16$ simplifies to 19. Thus, through a rigorous application of the order of operations, the expression is reduced to 19.

In the realm of algebra, particularly when dealing with intricate expressions that include variables, the PEMDAS rule remains an indispensable tool. For instance, when tasked with simplifying an expression such as $2(x + 3)^2 - 4$, the order of operations instructs us to initially focus on the operations contained within the Parentheses, specifically the expression $x + 3$. Given that the value of x is unspecified, further simplification within the parentheses is not feasible, prompting us to advance to Exponents, where $(x + 3)2$ is addressed. Subsequent steps involve any Multiplication or Division, followed by Addition or Subtraction. In this instance, the subtraction operation, represented by -4, constitutes the concluding step.

Mastery of PEMDAS necessitates a nuanced comprehension, particularly when Multiplication and Division or Addition and Subtraction are present sequentially within an expression. Take, for example, the expression $8 \div 2(2 + 2)$. The correct application of PEMDAS—executing division and multiplication from left to right—yields the calculation $8 \div 2 \times 4$, which simplifies to 4×4, resulting in 16. This underscores the critical importance of adhering to the prescribed sequence of operations to achieve accurate results.

Chapter 9: Linear Equations

9.1: Simplifying and Solving

Simplifying Expressions

Simplifying algebraic expressions is an essential skill in algebra, significantly impacting one's ability to solve linear equations efficiently and accurately. This process entails the meticulous combination of like terms and the precise distribution of coefficients across terms enclosed within parentheses. Developing proficiency in manipulating these expressions is of paramount importance for individuals preparing for the IBEW aptitude test, as it establishes the groundwork for tackling more intricate problem-solving scenarios prevalent in advanced mathematical contexts.

To delve deeper into the concept of "like terms," these are specific terms within an algebraic expression that possess identical variables raised to identical powers, thus allowing them to be combined. For example, consider the expression $2x + 3x$. Here, both terms qualify as like terms because they each contain the variable x raised to the power of one. The process of combining these like terms is methodical: one must perform the addition or subtraction of the coefficients associated with these terms. In this case, the expression $2x + 3x$ is simplified to $5x$ by adding the coefficients *2* and *3*, resulting in a single term with a coefficient of *5*.

The concept of distribution is rooted in the application of the distributive property, a fundamental algebraic principle that asserts that for any real numbers *a*, *b*, and *c*, the equation $a(b + c) = ab + ac$ is universally valid. This property becomes indispensable when dealing with expressions such as $3(x + 4)$. To simplify such an expression, one must distribute the coefficient, in this case, the number 3, across each term within the parentheses. This action results in the expression $3x + 12$, where *3* is multiplied by *x* and *3* is also multiplied by *4*, thereby transforming the original expression into its expanded form.

A frequent error encountered during the distribution process is the omission of applying the coefficient to every term contained within the parentheses. For instance, consider the expression $2(x - 3 + 4y)$. It is imperative to multiply the coefficient 2 by each individual term inside the parentheses, which includes *x*, *–3*, and *4y*. This careful application yields the expression $2x - 6 + 8y$, where each term is accurately scaled by the coefficient *2*.

An additional critical component of simplifying expressions involves the handling of subtraction and negative signs, which often require careful attention. Consider the expression $-3(x - 5y)$. In this instance, distributing the *–3* across the terms within the parentheses necessitates multiplying *–3* by each term, resulting in $-3x + 15y$. It is crucial to observe how the negative sign preceding the *3* impacts both terms during the distribution process, effectively altering their signs accordingly.

For individuals preparing for the IBEW aptitude test, achieving mastery of these techniques extends beyond the mere objective of passing the examination; it is about establishing a robust foundational understanding that will be instrumental in a future career within the electrical field. The ability to simplify expressions with efficiency enables the solving of more complex equations and facilitates comprehension of electrical formulas and calculations that are integral to the profession.

Solving Equations Step-by-Step

To solve equations, employing a systematic approach is imperative for isolating the variable and accurately determining its value. This methodological process is particularly vital for aspiring electricians preparing for the IBEW aptitude test, as it underpins much of the algebraic reasoning required within the electrical field.

One-step equations necessitate the execution of a singular mathematical operation to resolve. Consider the equation $x + 6+= 11$. The solution involves subtracting 6 from both sides, resulting in $x = 5$. The foundational principle here is to execute the inverse operation, in this case, subtraction, to isolate the variable while ensuring that the equation remains balanced on both sides of the equality. This balance is maintained by applying the same operation to both sides, thus preserving equality.

Two-step equations introduce an additional layer of complexity, requiring the execution of two distinct operations to achieve variable isolation. Take, for instance, the equation $2x + 3 = 9$. The initial step involves subtracting 3 from both sides, yielding $2x = 6$. Subsequently, dividing both sides by 2 derives $x = 3$. The strategic approach here involves reversing the operations that affect the variable, first addressing the additive or subtractive component and then tackling the multiplicative or divisive component, ensuring each step is performed symmetrically on both sides of the equation to maintain equilibrium.

Multi-step equations typically demand a sequence of operations, including distributing terms, combining like terms, and applying the properties of equality across several stages. For example, in the equation $3(2x - 4) + 5 = 11$, the initial task is to distribute the coefficient 3 across the terms within the parentheses, resulting in $6x - 12 + 5 = 11$. Simplifying this expression leads to $6x - 7 = 11$. Adding 7 to both sides yields $6x = 18$, and dividing by 6 finally isolates the variable, giving $x = 3$. This carefully structured approach tackles one operation at a time while rigorously maintaining the equation's balance, ensuring that each step logically follows from the previous one.

A common pitfall in the process of solving equations is neglecting the **distributive property** or mishandling **negative signs**. It is crucial to distribute coefficients thoroughly across all terms within parentheses and to vigilantly track the signs of each term when performing addition or subtraction throughout the equation. Mismanagement of these elements can lead to errors in calculation and incorrect solutions.

In equations where variables appear on both sides, such as $2x + 4 = x - 6$, the focus should be on relocating all variable terms to one side of the equation and all constant terms to the opposite side. By subtracting x from both sides and subsequently subtracting 4 from each side, you arrive at $x = -10$. This process underscores the significance of consolidating variable terms to one side, thereby simplifying the equation and facilitating the solution process.

9.2: Application and Strategy

Word Problems Solving with Equations

Mastering the skill of solving word problems involving linear equations is crucial for individuals preparing for the IBEW aptitude test, as it intricately links abstract mathematical concepts with their real-world applications, particularly in the electrical trade. To effectively address these problems, one must initiate the process by meticulously converting the given scenario into a corresponding algebraic equation, which subsequently allows for the determination of the unknown variable. This requires a careful extraction and identification of critical data points from the problem statement, followed by a thorough analysis of the mathematical relationships between these data points.

Consider a practical scenario where an electrician is tasked with determining the appropriate length of wire necessary for a specific project. The problem specifies: "An electrician requires a piece of wire that is twice as long as the distance between two power outlets, which are *15* feet apart. An extra 10 feet of wire is also needed for installation. How long does the wire need to be?" To solve this, let x denote the length of the wire needed. The distance between the outlets is given as *15* feet. Therefore, the wire must be 2×15 feet to satisfy the condition of being twice as long as this distance. Additionally, 10 feet of wire is required for installation purposes. This information translates into the algebraic equation $x = 2(15) + 10$. By performing the arithmetic operations, we first calculate $2 \times 15 = 30$, and then add the extra *10* feet, resulting in $x = 30 + 10$. Thus, $x = 40$ feet. Consequently, the electrician needs to procure a total of *40* feet of wire for the project.

In another illustrative example, consider a situation where it is necessary to determine the number of light fixtures an apprentice can install within a specified timeframe. The problem might state: "An apprentice can install 3 light fixtures per hour. If they have a 6-hour workday, how many fixtures can they install, assuming they work at a consistent pace and take a 30-minute lunch break?" Define y as the total number of fixtures installed by the apprentice. The apprentice's effective working time is calculated by subtracting the lunch break from the total workday, which is $6 - 0.5 = 5.5$ hours. The equation modeling this scenario is $y = 3 \times 5.5$. Solving for y, we perform the multiplication 3×5.5, yielding $y = 16.5$. Since it is impractical to install a fraction of a fixture, the maximum feasible number of complete fixtures the apprentice can install within the day is *16*.

Common Mistakes in Solving Equations

A frequent oversight in solving equations is the misapplication of the order of operations, particularly when dealing with equations that contain multiple terms and operations. For instance, consider an equation such as $3x + 2(x - 5) = 16$. The correct approach begins with the application of the distributive property, which necessitates multiplying the coefficient 2 by each term within the parentheses. This operation yields $3x + 2x - 10 = 16$. Following this, it is essential to combine like terms, specifically the terms involving x, resulting in $5x - 10 = 16$. The next critical step involves isolating the variable x. This is accomplished by adding 10 to both sides of the equation, adjusting it to $5x = 26$. Subsequently, dividing both sides by 5 allows for the determination of x, resulting in $x = \frac{26}{5}$ or equivalently $x = 5.2$. Neglecting the proper sequence of expanding the equation, combining like terms, and isolating the variable can lead to incorrect solutions.

A common mistake arises from failing to fully isolate the variable, a step that is crucial for accurately solving any equation. Consider the equation $4(x + 2) = 3x + 9$. To properly isolate x, it is necessary first to distribute the across both terms within the parentheses, resulting in the equation $4x + 8 = 3x + 9$. The subsequent step involves transferring all terms that contain the variable x to one side of the equation and all constant terms to the opposite side. This operation involves subtracting $3x$ from both sides, leading to $4x - 3x = 9 - 8$, which simplifies to $x = 1$. Any deviation from these steps, whether by omission or incorrect execution, can result in an erroneous conclusion.

Incorrectly handling fractions is another pitfall encountered in equation solving. In equations such as $\frac{1}{2}x + 3 = \frac{3}{4}x + 2$, the process of simplification can be facilitated by finding a common denominator for the fractions or, alternatively, multiplying every term by the least common multiple of the denominators, which in this case is 4. This operation transforms the equation into $2x + 12 = 3x + 8$. By clearing the fractions early in the process, the path to isolating x is simplified, ultimately revealing that $x = 4$. Neglecting the strategy of eliminating fractions at the outset can complicate the solution process and obscure the correct answer.

A subtle yet significant error occurs when students overlook the implications of dividing by a variable term, an oversight that can lead to the loss of potential solutions or result in division by zero. For equations involving terms such as $x(x - 5) = 0$, it is crucial to recognize that the equation is satisfied when $x = 0$ or $x = 5$. Prematurely dividing by x without considering $x = 0$ as a valid solution effectively eliminates a correct answer from consideration, as dividing by zero is undefined and invalidates this potential solution.

Chapter 10: Systems of Equations

10.1: Solving Techniques

What Are Systems? Solving Two Variables

In the realm of algebraic studies, a **system of equations** refers to a collection of two or more equations that incorporate the same set of variables. The primary objective when addressing such a system is to ascertain the specific values of these variables that will satisfy each equation simultaneously. This understanding is particularly crucial for individuals preparing for the IBEW aptitude test, as it directly correlates to practical applications in electrical engineering, such as determining the precise currents or voltages in electrical circuits that feature multiple loops, a common scenario in circuit analysis.

When approaching a system consisting of two equations, two primary techniques are often employed: **substitution** and **elimination**. Each method is designed to methodically reduce the complexity of the system by transforming it into a single equation that contains only one variable, which can then be resolved using established algebraic procedures.

Substitution Method:
1. Begin by isolating one of the variables in one of the equations. This involves manipulating the equation to express one variable explicitly in terms of the other variable. This step is essential as it sets the stage for substitution.

2. Substitute the expression obtained in the previous step into the second equation. This substitution effectively reduces the system to a single equation that involves only one variable, simplifying the problem by eliminating one of the variables.

3. Solve the resultant single-variable equation using appropriate algebraic techniques to determine the value of the isolated variable.

4. Substitute the value obtained back into the expression derived in the first step to calculate the value of the second variable, ensuring both variables are determined.

For example, consider the following system of equations:

$$x + y = 10$$

$$2x - y = 3$$

First, solve the initial equation for y, yielding $y = 10 - x$. Next, substitute this expression for y into the second equation, resulting in $2x - (10 - x) = 3$. Simplifying this yields $3x = 13$, and solving gives $x = \dfrac{13}{3}$. Substitute this value of x back into the expression $y = 10 - x$, resulting in $y = 10 - \dfrac{13}{3}$, which simplifies to $y = \dfrac{17}{3}$.

Elimination Method:

1. Adjust one or both of the original equations by multiplying them by a constant. This is done to create coefficients for one of the variables that are equal in magnitude but opposite in sign, facilitating their elimination through addition or subtraction.

2. Add or subtract the modified equations to eliminate one of the variables, thereby reducing the system to a single equation with only one variable remaining.

3. Solve the resultant equation for the remaining variable, using standard algebraic methods to find its value.

4. Substitute the value of the solved variable back into one of the original equations to ascertain the value of the other variable, ensuring that both variables are accounted for.

Applying this method to the same system, add the two equations directly to eliminate y:

$$x + y + 2x - y = 10 + 3$$

$$3x = 13$$

This results in $x = \dfrac{13}{3}$, and substituting this value back into one of the original equations, such as $x + y = 10$, will yield $y = \dfrac{17}{3}$.

Substitution & Elimination Methods

Mastering the techniques of **substitution** and **elimination** is crucial for the proficient resolution of systems of linear equations, a competency that is essential for aspiring electricians preparing for the International Brotherhood of Electrical Workers (IBEW) aptitude test. These methodologies are foundational in the comprehension of electrical circuit analysis, where each variable within the equations corresponds to specific electrical quantities such as voltage (V) and current (I), which are pivotal in circuit design and analysis.

The **substitution method** is particularly advantageous when one of the equations within the system can be manipulated to express one variable explicitly in terms of the other variable(s). This approach involves a series of precise steps:

1. **Isolate a variable:** Select an equation where a variable can be easily isolated. For example, given the equation $x + 2y = 6$, rearrange the terms to solve for x, resulting in the expression $x = 6 - 2y$. This step necessitates algebraic manipulation to express one variable explicitly, ensuring that the expression is in its simplest form for substitution.

2. **Substitute the expression:** Insert the isolated variable expression into the other equation in the system. If the second equation is $3x + y = 9$, replace x with the expression $6 - 2y$ to transform the equation into $3(6 - 2y) + y = 9$. This substitution step entails distributing and combining like terms to form a new equation that is solely in terms of one variable.

3. **Solve for the remaining variable:** Simplify the resulting equation to isolate the remaining variable. The equation $18 - 6y + y = 9$ simplifies to $18 - 5y = 9$, then further to

   $5y = 9$, ultimately yielding $y = \frac{9}{5}$. Once y is determined, substitute it back into one of the

   original equations to compute the value of x, ensuring consistency and accuracy in the solution across both equations.

The **elimination method** is effective when the system of equations allows for the direct elimination of one variable through addition or subtraction. This method comprises the following detailed steps:

1. **Align coefficients:** Adjust the coefficients of one variable in the equations by multiplying one or both equations by a strategically chosen factor. For instance, given the system $2x + 3y = 5$ and $4x - y = 11$, multiply the second equation by 3 to make the coefficients of y equal, resulting in the new equation $12x - 3y = 33$.

2. **Add or subtract the equations:** Combine the modified equations to eliminate one variable. By adding the equations $2x + 3y = 5$ and $12x - 3y = 33$, the y terms cancel out, yielding $14x = 38$. This step requires careful attention to ensure that the variables align correctly for effective elimination.

3. **Solve for the remaining variable:** Isolate the remaining variable by solving the

   simplified equation. From $14x = 38$, solve for x to find $x = \frac{38}{14}$, which reduces to $x = \frac{19}{7}$.

   Substitute this value back into one of the original equations to determine the corresponding value of , verifying the solution through back-substitution.

A methodical approach to **manipulating** and **simplifying** equations is essential for the successful application of both substitution and elimination methods. The decision to employ either method is contingent upon the structure of the given system of equations and which approach provides the most direct and efficient pathway to the solution. Mastery of both methods equips test-takers with the versatility to address a broad spectrum of problems, ensuring readiness for questions that involve complex circuit calculations and other applications in electrical engineering. Engaging with a diverse array of practice problems hones the ability to swiftly identify the optimal strategy, a vital skill for both the aptitude test and practical electrical work.

10.2 : Visual & Real-World Applications

Graphical Solutions

Graphical solutions provide an explicit and intuitive method for resolving systems of equations by utilizing visual representations on a coordinate plane, where the intersection points of the graphs correspond to the solutions of the system. This approach is particularly advantageous for analyzing the interdependencies between variables in complex real-world scenarios, such as the analysis of electrical circuits. In such circuits, the relationship between voltage and current can be influenced by varying resistances and the configuration of the circuit pathways, rendering graphical solutions an insightful tool for visualizing these interactions.

To graphically solve a system of equations, each equation is represented as a distinct line on a Cartesian coordinate plane. The Cartesian plane, defined by its x-axis and y-axis, serves as the framework where each line is plotted based on the equation's slope and y-intercept. The coordinates at which two lines intersect on this plane represent the specific values of the variables that satisfy both equations simultaneously. The precision of graphing each equation is crucial, as even a slight error can lead to misinterpretation of the intersection points and, consequently, incorrect solutions.

Consider the following system of linear equations:

$$y = 2x + 3$$

$$y = -x + 5$$

To begin graphing, identify the y-intercept for each equation, which is the point where the line crosses the y-axis. For the first equation, $y = 2x + 3$, the y-intercept is at the point (0, 3). For the second equation, $y = -x + 5$, the y-intercept is at the point (0, 5). Next, use the slope to determine an additional point on each line. The slope of the first equation is 2, indicating that for every increment of 1 unit in the x-direction, the y-value increases by 2 units. This can be visualized by starting at the y-intercept (0, 3) and moving 1 unit to the right along the x-axis to reach the point (1, 5) on the line. For the second equation, the slope is -1, signifying that for each unit increase in the x-direction, the y-value decreases by 1 unit. From the y-intercept (0, 5), move 1 unit to the right to reach the point (1, 4) on the line.

Upon completing the graphing of both lines on the Cartesian plane, the next step is to identify the intersection point of the two lines. For the given equations, the lines intersect at the coordinate point (1, 5). This intersection point denotes that when $x = 1$, both equations yield the same y-value of 5, thereby providing the solution to the system of equations.

When analyzing intersection points, several key concepts are essential:

- **Consistency:** The presence of intersecting lines on the graph signifies a consistent system, indicating that at least one solution exists where the equations simultaneously hold true.

- **Inconsistency:** If the lines are parallel and do not intersect at any point, the system is inconsistent, meaning there are no values of x and y that satisfy both equations.

- **Dependence:** When the lines coincide, meaning they overlap completely, the system is dependent, suggesting that an infinite number of solutions exist, as all points on the line satisfy both equations.

In practical applications, graphical representations offer a powerful means to visualize and comprehend the effect of one variable on another. For instance, in electrical circuits, graphing can illustrate how modifications in resistance, represented by one equation, impact the current flow, represented by another equation, under varying circuit conditions. This visualization aids engineers and scientists in predicting and optimizing circuit behavior.

Application Problems

In the specialized domain of electrical engineering, the application of systems of equations to practical scenarios is crucial for precise circuit analysis and design. Consider a common problem encountered by electricians, which involves determining the total resistance in a circuit configuration that includes resistors arranged in both parallel and series configurations. This task necessitates a methodical approach to accurately compute resistance values, which are fundamental to predicting circuit behavior.

Envision a circuit in which two resistors, denoted as R_1 and R_2, are configured in parallel within one segment of the circuit. In conjunction with this parallel arrangement, a third resistor, R_3, is connected in series. The objective is to calculate the overall resistance of the circuit, referred to as R_{total}. The procedure begins by calculating the equivalent resistance of the parallel resistor combination, termed $R_{parallel}$. This value is then combined with the resistance of the series resistor, R_3, to yield the total circuit resistance.

The mathematical expression for determining the equivalent resistance of resistors arranged in parallel is given by the reciprocal formula:

$$\frac{1}{R_{parallel}} = \frac{1}{R_1} + \frac{1}{R_2}$$

This formula is derived from the principle that the reciprocal of the total equivalent resistance of parallel resistors equals the sum of the reciprocals of each individual resistor's resistance.

For resistors connected in series, the total resistance is calculated by the straightforward summation of their individual resistances:

$$R_{total} = R_{parallel} + R_3$$

This is based on the principle that resistors in series simply add up, as the same current flows through each resistor sequentially.

Example Problem:
Suppose you have specific resistance values: $R_1 = 4\Omega$, $R_2 = 6\Omega$, and $R_3 = 10\Omega$. The task is to compute the total resistance across the entire circuit.

Solution:
1. Calculate $R_{parallel}$:

    Begin by determining the reciprocal of the equivalent resistance for the parallel portion:
    $$\frac{1}{R_{parallel}} = \frac{1}{4} + \frac{1}{6}$$

    Convert each term to a common denominator, which in this case is 12, to facilitate the addition:
    $$\frac{1}{4} = \frac{3}{12}, \quad \frac{1}{6} = \frac{2}{12}$$

    Adding these fractions yields:
    $$\frac{3}{12} + \frac{2}{12} = \frac{5}{12}$$

    To find $R_{parallel}$, take the reciprocal of the sum:
    $$R_{parallel} = \frac{12}{5}\Omega$$

2. Compute R_{total}:

    The next step involves adding $R_{parallel}$ to the resistance of the series resistor, R_3:

    $$R_{total} = R_{parallel} + R_3$$

    Substitute the known values:

    $$R_{total} = \frac{12}{5} + 10$$

Convert *10* to a fraction with a denominator of *5* for consistency:

$$10 = \frac{50}{5}$$

Add these fractions:

$$\frac{12}{5} + \frac{50}{5} = \frac{62}{5}\Omega$$

Convert the result to a decimal for practical use:

$$R_{total} = 12.4\Omega$$

Chapter 11: Quadratic Equations

11.1 : Solving Quadratics

Recognizing Quadratics

The identification and understanding of quadratic equations are essential for their effective resolution. A quadratic equation can be expressed in the canonical form $ax^2 + bx + c = 0$, where the coefficients a, b, and c are constants, and critically, a must not equal zero, as this ensures the presence of the quadratic term. The term ax^2 is the quadratic term, which is responsible for the parabolic nature of the graph of the equation. The linear term, bx, contributes to the slope of the parabola at the vertex, while the constant term c determines the point at which the parabola intersects the y-axis. The distinguishing feature of quadratic equations is the presence of the x^2 term, which sets them apart from linear equations, which lack this term, and from higher-degree polynomial equations, which include terms with exponents greater than 2.

A thorough understanding of the standard form of a quadratic equation is imperative, as it facilitates the application of various solution techniques, including factoring, completing the square, and employing the quadratic formula. The coefficient a plays a pivotal role in determining the geometry of the parabola described by the quadratic equation. Specifically, the magnitude of a affects the parabola's width; a larger absolute value of a results in a narrower parabola, while a smaller absolute value results in a wider one. The sign of a dictates the parabola's orientation: a positive indicates that the parabola opens upwards, resembling a U-shape, whereas a negative a causes the parabola to open downwards, forming an inverted U-shape. The vertex, which is the point of maximum or minimum value on the parabola, is influenced by both a and b and is calculated using the formula $(-b/(2a), f(-b/(2a)))$, where $f(x)$ represents the quadratic function. The y-intercept, determined solely by the constant term c, is the point where the graph crosses the y-axis, occurring at $(0, c)$.

To ascertain whether an equation is quadratic, one must examine the highest power of x present in the equation; if the highest power is 2, the equation is classified as quadratic. Quadratic equations can have a varied number of real solutions: zero, one, or two, which correspond to the x-intercepts of the parabola. The nature and quantity of these solutions are dictated by the discriminant, given by $b2 - 4ac$. A positive discriminant signifies two distinct real solutions, indicating that the parabola intersects the x-axis at two points. A discriminant of zero corresponds to a single real solution, where the vertex of the parabola touches the x-axis, implying the parabola is tangent to the x-axis at that point. A negative discriminant indicates the absence of real solutions, signifying that the parabola does not intersect the x-axis at any point, and the solutions are complex.

Factoring & Quadratic Formula

The process of solving quadratic equations constitutes an essential competency in algebra, particularly for individuals preparing for the International Brotherhood of Electrical Workers (IBEW) aptitude test. The two primary techniques employed for solving these equations are factoring and the application of the quadratic formula. Mastery of the conditions under which each method is most applicable can significantly enhance the efficiency and accuracy of problem-solving efforts.

Factoring involves the transformation of a quadratic equation of the form $ax2 + bx + c = 0$ into a product of two binomials. This method is most effective when the quadratic can be decomposed into factors without difficulty. For example, in the equation $x2 - 5x + 6 = 0$, the objective is to identify two integers that multiply to yield the constant term c (which is 6) and simultaneously sum to the coefficient b (which is -5). In this particular case, the integers -2 and -3 satisfy these conditions, as their product $(-2) \times (-3)$ equals 6, while their sum $(-2) + (-3)$ equals -5. Consequently, the equation can be expressed in its factored form as $(x - 2)(x - 3) = 0$, from which the solutions $x = 2$ and $x = 3$ are derived by setting each binomial equal to zero and solving for x.

In instances where quadratic equations are resistant to straightforward factoring, particularly those with large coefficients or those that do not decompose into neat factors, the quadratic formula provides a universally applicable solution. The formula is derived through the method of completing the square for the general form of a quadratic equation, and is represented as:

$$x = \frac{-b \pm \sqrt{b^2 - 4ac}}{2a}$$

This formula is comprehensive, guaranteeing solutions for any quadratic equation, including those with complex roots. To illustrate its application, consider the quadratic equation $2x^2 - 4x - 1 = 0$, where the coefficients are given as $a = 2$, $b = -4$, and $c = -1$. By substituting these values into the quadratic formula, we obtain:

$$x = \frac{-(-4) \pm \sqrt{(-4)^2 - 4(2)(-1)}}{2(2)}$$

This simplifies to:

$$x = \frac{4 \pm \sqrt{16 + 8}}{4} = \frac{4 \pm \sqrt{24}}{4}$$

Further simplification of $\sqrt{24}$ results in $2\sqrt{6}$, yielding the solutions:

$$x = \frac{4 \pm 2\sqrt{6}}{4} = 1 \pm \frac{\sqrt{6}}{2}$$

These solutions demonstrate the robustness of the quadratic formula in addressing equations that are not amenable to factoring, thereby highlighting its indispensability in solving complex quadratic equations.

Completing the Square

Completing the square is a mathematical procedure specifically designed to address quadratic equations that do not readily lend themselves to straightforward factorization. The method involves transforming a given quadratic equation into an equivalent equation featuring a perfect square trinomial, thereby streamlining the process of finding its solutions. Consider a quadratic equation presented in the standard form $ax^2 + bx + c = 0$. The objective is to manipulate this equation such that the terms involving x^2 and x are restructured into a perfect square expression.

Initially, it is crucial to ensure that the coefficient of the quadratic term, a, is normalized to 1. This normalization is achieved by dividing the entire equation by the coefficient a if it differs from 1. For example, given the quadratic equation $2x^2 + 4x - 6 = 0$, the entire equation must be divided by 2. This operation yields $x^2 + 2x - 3 = 0$, effectively standardizing the coefficient of the x^2 term to 1, which is essential for the subsequent steps.

The next step involves isolating the terms containing x by transposing the constant term c to the opposite side of the equation. In the case of $x^2 + 2x - 3 = 0$, adding 3 to both sides results in the equation $x^2 + 2x = 3$. This adjustment prepares the left side of the equation for the completion of the square.

To complete the square, it is necessary to identify a specific value that, when added to both sides of the equation, transforms the left side into a perfect square trinomial. This value is determined by taking half of the linear coefficient b (expressed as $b/2$), squaring it, and adding the resulting square to both sides of the equation. In the equation $x^2 + 2x = 3$, the linear coefficient b is 2. Dividing this by 2 yields 1, and squaring 1 results in 1. Consequently, adding 1 to both sides modifies the equation to $x^2 + 2x + 1 = 4$.

The left-hand side of the equation now represents a perfect square trinomial, specifically $(x + 1)^2$, which is equal to the right-hand side, 4. This transformation simplifies the equation to $(x + 1)^2 = 4$.

To solve for x, extract the square root of both sides of the equation, which results in two potential solutions due to the nature of square roots. From the equation $(x + 1)2 = 4$, taking the square root of both sides provides $x + 1 =)2$. Solving for x involves isolating it by subtracting 1 from both possible solutions, yielding the values $x = 1$ and $x = -3$.

11.2 : Graphing Quadratics

Parabolas: Graphs and Analysis

Understanding the graphical representation of a quadratic equation, which manifests as a parabola, is essential for effectively solving algebraic problems and interpreting various real-world phenomena. The critical characteristics of a parabola include the vertex, the axis of symmetry, and the x-intercepts, also referred to as roots.

The vertex of a parabola is a pivotal point that signifies either the peak or the trough of the graph, contingent on whether the parabola opens upwards or downwards. This point represents the maximum or minimum value of the quadratic function, respectively. The coordinates of the vertex can be precisely determined using the formula $(-\frac{b}{2a}, f(-\frac{b}{2a}))$. In this formula, a and b are coefficients derived from the standard form of the quadratic equation, expressed as $y = ax^2 + bx + c$. Here, $-\frac{b}{2a}$ calculates the x-coordinate of the vertex, which serves as the point of symmetry along the x-axis, while $f(-\frac{b}{2a})$ provides the corresponding y-coordinate by substituting back into the quadratic equation.

The axis of symmetry is a vertical line that intersects the vertex, effectively dividing the parabola into two congruent halves that are mirror images of one another. The mathematical equation representing this axis is $x = -\frac{b}{2a}$. This line is instrumental in analyzing the symmetric nature of a parabola, which is essential when solving quadratic equations graphically. The axis of symmetry offers insight into the equilibrium of the parabola, as each point on one side has a corresponding point on the opposite side at an equal distance from this axis.

The x-intercepts, or roots of the quadratic equation, are the points at which the graph crosses the x-axis. These intercepts are solutions to the quadratic equation $ax2 + bx + c = 0$. To ascertain these intercepts, one must set $y = 0$ and solve the resulting equation for x. This can be achieved through various techniques such as factoring, completing the square, or employing the quadratic formula. The discriminant, denoted as $b^2 - 4ac$, is a critical component in determining the nature of the roots. A positive discriminant indicates the presence of two distinct real solutions, resulting in two x-intercepts. A discriminant of zero implies a single real solution, meaning the vertex itself lies on the x-axis. Conversely, a negative discriminant signifies the absence of real solutions, indicating that the parabola does not intersect the x-axis.

When graphing a parabola, the process begins with plotting the vertex on the coordinate plane. Next, the axis of symmetry is drawn as a dashed vertical line passing through the vertex to visually represent the parabola's symmetry. If x-intercepts exist, they should be plotted accurately on the x-axis. Following these steps, the parabola can be sketched, ensuring that it opens upwards if the coefficient a is greater than zero, and downwards if a is less than zero. The symmetry about the axis of symmetry must be carefully maintained to ensure the graph's accuracy and to reflect the inherent properties of the quadratic function.

Chapter 12: Polynomials & Factoring

12.1 : Working with Polynomials

Understanding Polynomials

Polynomials are fundamental constructs in algebra, functioning as expressions that systematically integrate variables and constants through operations such as addition, subtraction, multiplication, and the application of non-negative integer exponents. To delve into the nature of polynomials, one must analyze their individual components and intrinsic characteristics, which are pivotal in the resolution of algebraic equations and are indispensable for individuals preparing for the IBEW aptitude test.

A polynomial expression is typically represented in the canonical form.

$$P(x) = a_n x^n + a_{n-1} x^{n-1} + \dots + a_1 x + a_0$$

In this notation, n represents a non-negative integer, and $a_n, a_{n-1}, \dots, a_1, a_0$ are constants, with the stipulation that $a_n \neq 0$. The variable x serves as the placeholder that the coefficients multiply. These constants are referred to as coefficients, with a_n designated as the leading coefficient because it is associated with the term containing the highest power of x. The degree of the polynomial, denoted by n, is defined as the greatest exponent of x present in the expression, and it plays a critical role in determining various properties of the polynomial.

The degree of a polynomial is a determinant of the configuration of its graph and the potential number of roots or solutions it may possess. For instance, a linear polynomial of degree one, such as $P(x) = 2x + 1$, graphically manifests as a straight line due to its first-degree nature. Conversely, a quadratic polynomial of degree two, exemplified by $P(x) = x2 - 4x + 4$, takes the form of a parabola when plotted on a graph, a direct consequence of its second-degree characteristic.

The leading coefficient exerts a substantial influence on the end behavior of the polynomial. Specifically, it dictates the asymptotic behavior of the polynomial as x approaches either positive or negative infinity. When a polynomial possesses a positive leading coefficient coupled with an even degree, the polynomial's graph will ultimately ascend towards positive infinity as x increases. In contrast, a negative leading coefficient will result in the polynomial's graph descending towards negative infinity under identical conditions of degree parity.

For candidates preparing for the IBEW aptitude test, proficiency in handling polynomials necessitates the rapid identification of both the degree and the leading coefficient, as these elements are crucial in formulating strategies for factoring, graphing, and solving polynomial equations. The ability to discern patterns within polynomial expressions can significantly streamline complex problem-solving processes, rendering them more manageable and less time-intensive.

This comprehension not only aids in test preparation but also establishes a robust groundwork for subsequent coursework and professional challenges in electrical work, where mathematical computations frequently underpin technical operations and problem-solving scenarios.

Adding & Subtracting: Combine Like Terms

Mastering the addition and subtraction of polynomials necessitates a detailed understanding of accurately combining like terms, which are defined as terms that possess identical variables elevated to identical powers. This level of precision is essential for the effective simplification of polynomial expressions and is critical when solving polynomial equations.

To add or subtract polynomials, follow these detailed steps:

1. **Identify Like Terms:** Thoroughly examine each polynomial expression to locate terms that share the exact same variable(s) and exponent. This involves a meticulous comparison of each term's structure. For example, consider the polynomial expression $3x^2 + 5x - 2 + 4x^2 - 3x$. In this case, the terms $3x^2$ and $4x^2$ are categorized as like terms because they both contain the variable x raised to the power of 2. Similarly, the terms $5x$ and $-3x$ are like terms as they both consist of the variable raised to the first power. It is crucial to ensure that the exponents are identical; otherwise, the terms cannot be combined.

2. **Combine Coefficients:** Once the like terms have been identified, the subsequent step involves the arithmetic operation of adding or subtracting their coefficients. This requires a precise calculation to ensure accuracy. In the aforementioned example, the coefficients of the like terms $3x^2$ and $4x^2$ are combined to yield $7x^2$. Similarly, the coefficients of $5x$ and $-3x$ are combined to result in $2x$. It is important to include any constant terms present in the polynomial expressions. In this instance, there is a single constant term, -2, which remains unchanged as there are no other constants to combine.

3. **Write the Simplified Expression:** After combining the like terms, it is essential to meticulously document the resulting simplified expression. From our example, the simplified expression is $7x^2 + 2x - 2$. This step involves ensuring that all terms are accurately accounted for and that the expression is presented in a clear and organized manner.

It is imperative to combine only like terms, as combining terms with different exponents, such as x^2 and x, is not permissible due to their distinct exponential values. This process is not only vital for simplifying expressions but also serves as the foundational groundwork for more complex polynomial operations, including multiplication and division. The ability to recognize and accurately combine like terms is a critical step in these operations. Developing proficiency in the addition and subtraction of polynomials through the precise combination of like terms is a fundamental skill that will enhance your performance on the IBEW aptitude test and in your future electrical career, where precise mathematical solutions are often necessary to address technical challenges.

12.2: Multiplication and Factoring

Multiplying Polynomials with FOIL Method

The FOIL method is an essential technique for the multiplication of binomials, a fundamental skill for individuals preparing for the IBEW aptitude test. This method, encapsulated by the acronym First, Outer, Inner, Last, provides a systematic approach to ensure that all components of each binomial are accurately multiplied. The execution of the FOIL method involves a precise sequence of operations: first, multiply the First terms of each binomial; then proceed to the Outer terms, followed by the Inner terms, and finally, the Last terms. The results obtained from these multiplications are subsequently aggregated to yield the resultant polynomial.

Consider the multiplication of two specific binomials, *(x + 3)* and *(x – 2)*. The application of the FOIL method mandates the following detailed steps:

1. **First (F):** Begin by multiplying the first terms from each binomial. In this instance, it involves the operation $x \cdot x$, resulting in x^2. This step is crucial as it establishes the degree of the resulting polynomial.

2. **Outer (O):** Next, focus on the multiplication of the outermost terms. Here, the calculation is $x \cdot (-2)$, yielding $-2x$. This step addresses the interaction between the leading term of the first binomial and the trailing term of the second binomial.

3. **Inner (I):** Subsequently, multiply the inner terms. This involves $3 \cdot x$, resulting in $3x$. This step captures the interaction between the trailing term of the first binomial and the leading term of the second binomial.

4. **Last (L):** Finally, multiply the last terms of each binomial. The operation $3 \cdot (-2)$ results in -6. This step completes the multiplication process by addressing the interaction of the trailing terms of both binomials.

Upon executing these operations, the results are combined to form the expression $x^2 - 2x + 3x - 6$. The next step involves simplifying this expression by combining like terms, specifically the linear terms $-2x$ and $3x$, which sum to x. Consequently, the simplified polynomial expression is $x^2 + x - 6$.

The FOIL method not only facilitates the multiplication of binomials but also reinforces comprehension of the distributive property. This is evident as each term in the first binomial is systematically multiplied by each term in the second binomial, ensuring comprehensive coverage of all possible products. The method's straightforwardness and efficiency render it an invaluable tool for test-takers who must solve problems with precision under stringent time constraints.

Mastery of the FOIL method is achieved through consistent practice. Engaging with a variety of binomial multiplication exercises enhances one's proficiency in swiftly and accurately applying the FOIL steps, thereby augmenting problem-solving speed and efficiency. This skill is advantageous not only for the IBEW aptitude test but also for subsequent coursework and professional challenges in the field of electrical work, where precise mathematical calculations are frequently required.

Factoring Trinomials and Special Identities

Factoring trinomials and recognizing special identities are essential skills for candidates preparing for the IBEW aptitude test, as they facilitate the simplification of algebraic expressions and the efficient resolution of equations. A trinomial, defined as a specific type of polynomial comprised of three distinct terms, is generally expressed in the form $ax^2 + bx + c$, where each of a, b, and c represents a constant coefficient. The primary objective in this context is to decompose the trinomial into the product of two binomial expressions, represented as *(dx + e)(fx + g)*, thereby streamlining the process of solving algebraic expressions.

The procedure for factoring a trinomial involves identifying two specific numbers that simultaneously fulfill two conditions: their product must equal the product of the coefficients and , and their sum must equal the coefficient b. This dual-condition requirement can be particularly challenging within the constraints of a timed test environment; however, through repeated practice, one can discern patterns that make the task more intuitive. For example, consider the trinomial $x^2 + 5x + 6$; in this case, the numbers 2 and 3 not only sum to 5 but also multiply to yield 6, leading to the factorization of the trinomial into the binomials *(x + 2)(x + 3)*.

Special identities serve as strategic formulas that provide efficient pathways for factoring specific categories of polynomials. These identities are critical tools, particularly when addressing intricate polynomials or simplifying expressions prior to equation solving. Three pivotal identities to commit to memory include:

1. **Square of a Sum:** The identity $(a+b)^2 = a^2 + 2ab + b^2$ offers a direct method for expanding squared binomials, transforming them into a trinomial format.

2. **Square of a Difference:** The identity $(a-b)^2 = a^2 - 2ab + b^2$ similarly provides a formulaic approach to expanding squared binomials where subtraction is involved.

3. **Difference of Squares:** The identity $a^2 - b^2 = (a+b)(a-b)$ enables the immediate factorization of expressions that conform to the difference of squares pattern, which is particularly useful for simplifying and solving equations.

These identities are especially advantageous when managing complex polynomial expressions or when simplification of expressions is necessary before proceeding to solve equations. For instance, recognizing the expression $x^2 - 9$ as a difference of squares permits its straightforward factorization into $(x + 3)(x - 3)$, thereby illustrating the power and utility of these algebraic shortcuts.

Chapter 13: Rational Expressions

13.1: Core Operations

Rational Expressions Defined

Rational expressions are a specific category of algebraic fractions characterized by having both the numerator and the denominator composed of polynomial expressions. These polynomials can vary in complexity, ranging from simple constants to intricate expressions containing multiple terms and higher-degree variables. The archetypal representation of a rational expression is given by $\frac{p(x)}{q(x)}$, where $q(x) \neq 0$ is a critical condition to prevent the undefined scenario of division by zero, which would otherwise invalidate the expression.

The structure of rational expressions involves two primary components: the **numerator** $p(x)$ and the **denominator** $q(x)$. The numerator, serving as the dividend, is the polynomial expression positioned above the fraction bar, while the denominator, functioning as the divisor, is the polynomial located below the fraction bar. These components can range from simple monomials like *3x* to more complex polynomials such as $x^3 - 4x^2 + x - 7$. For instance, in the expression $\frac{x^2 + 2x + 1}{x - 3}$, the numerator $x^2 + 2x + 1$ is classified as a quadratic polynomial, while the denominator $x - 3$ is identified as a linear polynomial.

A comprehensive understanding of rational expressions is essential for executing operations such as solving equations and simplifying expressions. These expressions undergo various algebraic manipulations, including addition, subtraction, multiplication, and division. Each operation necessitates a distinct method to ensure the integrity of mathematical relationships.

Simplifying rational expressions involves reducing them to their simplest form by factoring both the numerator and the denominator to identify and cancel out any common factors. For example, consider the expression $\frac{x^2 - 9}{x^2 - 4x + 4}$. The numerator $x^2 - 9$ can be factored into $(x+3)(x-3)$, and the denominator $x^2 - 4x + 4$ can be factored into $(x-2)^2$. This simplification process results in the expression $\frac{(x+3)(x-3)}{(x-2)^2}$.

When engaging in multiplication and division of rational expressions, the process involves multiplying the numerators together and the denominators together. In division, it is necessary to take the reciprocal of the second fraction before proceeding with multiplication. For instance, to divide $\dfrac{a(x)}{b(x)}$ by $\dfrac{c(x)}{d(x)}$, one would multiply $\dfrac{a(x)}{b(x)}$ by $\dfrac{d(x)}{c(x)}$.

For addition and subtraction of rational expressions, it is imperative to first establish a common denominator. This often involves determining the least common denominator (LCD) of the expressions involved. Each fraction must be adjusted by multiplying the numerator and denominator by the necessary factors to achieve the LCD before performing the addition or subtraction operation.

Rational expressions are prevalent in various forms on the IBEW aptitude test, presenting a range of challenges from simplifying intricate expressions to solving algebraic equations and comprehending functional relationships. Mastery of these expressions equips test-takers with the skills necessary to approach and resolve a broad spectrum of algebraic problems effectively.

Simplifying: Factor and Reduce

Simplifying rational expressions to their most reduced form is a crucial technique that enhances clarity and efficiency in navigating complex algebraic problems. This process necessitates a meticulous approach to factorization, beginning with the numerator and followed by the denominator, and then systematically reducing the expression by eliminating any common factors.

Examine the rational expression $\dfrac{x^2 - 4}{x^2 - 5x + 4}$. Initially, the numerator $x^2 - 4$ is recognized as a difference of squares, a specific algebraic identity. This identity states that $a^2 - b^2$ can be factored into $(a + b)(a - b)$. Applying this to $x^2 - 4$, where $a = x$ and $b = 2$, results in the factorization $(x + 2)(x - 2)$.

Turning attention to the denominator $x^2 - 5x + 4$, the objective is to factor this quadratic expression. This involves identifying two numbers whose product equals the constant term and whose sum equals the linear coefficient -5. Through trial or systematic analysis, the numbers -4 and -1 fulfill these conditions, leading to the factorization $(x - 4)(x - 1)$.

Thus, the expression in its factored form becomes $\dfrac{(x + 2)(x - 2)}{(x - 4)(x - 1)}$. A thorough inspection reveals no common factors between the numerator and the denominator, indicating that the expression is already in its simplest form. Despite this, the process of factoring and attempting reduction is indispensable for confirming the expression is indeed simplified.

Consider a scenario where common factors exist, as in the expression $\dfrac{x^2 - 9}{x^2 - 3x - 18}$. First, the numerator $x^2 - 9$ is identified as a difference of squares, factorable into $(x + 3)(x - 3)$. For the denominator $x^2 - 3x - 18$, the task is to identify two numbers that multiply to -18 and add to -3.

The numbers 3 and –6 meet these criteria, resulting in the factorization $(x-6)(x+3)$.

In this case, the factor $x+3$ appears in both the numerator and the denominator, allowing it to be cancelled out. This reduction simplifies the expression to $\frac{(x-3)}{(x-6)}$, demonstrating the importance of recognizing and eliminating common factors.

To simplify rational expressions effectively, adhere to these detailed steps:

1. Factor both the numerator and the denominator into their most basic components, considering algebraic identities such as the difference of squares, perfect square trinomials, or the sum and difference of cubes.
2. Meticulously identify any common factors present between the numerator and the denominator, ensuring that no potential simplification is overlooked.
3. Cancel out these common factors, rewriting the expression in its reduced form, provided that such reduction is feasible.

Developing proficiency in these steps ensures that rational expressions are simplified accurately, which is crucial for the efficient manipulation and resolution of algebraic equations. This skill is particularly valuable in high-stakes contexts such as the IBEW aptitude test, where both efficiency and precision are critical. Engaging in regular practice with a diverse array of expressions fosters familiarity and confidence, transforming a potentially complex task into a manageable component of algebraic problem-solving.

13.2: Arithmetic and Solving

Multiplying & Dividing: Cross-Cancellation

Multiplying and dividing rational expressions necessitate a systematic and methodical approach to ensure the simplification of the expressions while maintaining the precision of calculations. Cross-cancellation is a technique employed to optimize this process by identifying and eliminating common factors present between the numerators and denominators prior to executing the multiplication or division operations. This method is essential in minimizing the potential for computational errors, thereby making it a crucial skill for individuals preparing for the International Brotherhood of Electrical Workers (IBEW) aptitude test, where accuracy and efficiency in mathematical problem-solving are paramount.

When engaging in the multiplication of rational expressions, the initial step involves a thorough examination of both the numerators and denominators to detect any common factors that can be canceled out. Consider the multiplication of the rational expressions $\frac{2x}{3y}$ and $\frac{9y}{4x}$.

In this instance, a detailed inspection reveals that both the variable x in the numerator of the first expression and the denominator of the second expression, as well as the variable y in the denominator of the first expression and the numerator of the second expression, are common factors. By applying cross-cancellation, these common factors are eliminated, resulting in the simplified multiplication of $\frac{2}{3} \times \frac{9}{4}$. This expression can be further simplified to $\frac{18}{12}$, which reduces to $\frac{3}{2}$ after dividing both the numerator and the denominator by their greatest common divisor, which is 6.

In the context of dividing rational expressions, the procedure involves an additional step of taking the reciprocal of the divisor, thereby transforming the division operation into a multiplication operation. For example, when dividing $\frac{x^2-4}{x-2}$ by $\frac{x^2-x-6}{x^2-9}$, the division is converted into the multiplication of $\frac{x^2-4}{x-2}$ by the reciprocal of the divisor, which is $\frac{x^2-9}{x^2-x-6}$. This transformation necessitates the factoring of each polynomial expression. The expression $\frac{x^2-4}{x-2}$ is factored into $\frac{(x+2)(x-2)}{x-2}$, while the expression $\frac{x^2-9}{x^2-x-6}$ is factored into $\frac{(x+3)(x-3)}{(x-3)(x+2)}$. Upon factoring, it becomes evident that the factors $(x-2)$, $(x+2)$, and $(x-3)$ are common between the numerators and denominators, allowing for cross-cancellation. The expression simplifies to $\frac{1}{x-3}$ after canceling these common factors, illustrating the efficacy of cross-cancellation in streamlining the division of rational expressions.

A comprehensive understanding of factoring polynomials and the ability to swiftly recognize common factors are indispensable for the effective application of cross-cancellation. This technique plays a pivotal role in simplifying complex rational expressions and ensures that solutions are presented in their simplest form. Developing proficiency in cross-cancellation can substantially enhance the efficiency with which algebraic problems involving the multiplication and division of rational expressions are solved, particularly for those who aspire to achieve excellence in the IBEW aptitude test. Engaging in regular practice with a diverse range of expressions is essential for cultivating the intuitive application of cross-cancellation.

Adding & Subtracting Expressions

To perform addition and subtraction on rational expressions, the crucial initial step involves identifying a common denominator, similar to the process utilized when dealing with simple fractions. This requires determining the Least Common Denominator (LCD), which is defined as the smallest multiple shared by the denominators of the expressions in question. The process of finding the LCD involves analyzing the structure of each denominator, identifying all distinct factors, and subsequently constructing the smallest expression that includes each factor the maximum number of times it appears in any denominator. Once the LCD is identified, each rational expression must be adjusted by multiplying both its numerator and denominator by the necessary factors to transform its denominator into the LCD, thereby ensuring that all expressions share a common base for accurate combination.

Consider the rational expressions $\frac{3}{x}$ and $\frac{4}{y}$. Here, x and y are distinct variables that do not share any common factors; thus, the LCD is the product of these variables, specifically xy. To adjust each fraction to have this common denominator, multiply the numerator and denominator of $\frac{3}{x}$ by the missing factor y, resulting in $\frac{3y}{xy}$. Similarly, multiply the numerator and denominator of $\frac{4}{y}$ by the missing factor x, resulting in $\frac{4x}{xy}$.

For the addition of these expressions, the procedure is as follows:

$$\frac{3}{x}+\frac{4}{y}=\frac{3y}{xy}+\frac{4x}{xy}=\frac{3y+4x}{xy}$$

For their subtraction, the process is:

$$\frac{3}{x}-\frac{4}{y}=\frac{3y}{xy}-\frac{4x}{xy}=\frac{3y-4x}{xy}$$

The detailed steps for adding and subtracting rational expressions are as follows:

1. **Determine the LCD** by finding the least common multiple of all denominators involved. This involves factoring each denominator into its prime components and constructing the smallest expression that contains each factor the greatest number of times it appears in any one denominator.

2. **Modify the expressions** by multiplying both the numerator and denominator of each rational expression by the factors necessary to achieve the LCD as the new denominator. This ensures that all expressions have equivalent denominators and can be directly combined.

3. **Combine the numerators** of the rational expressions by either adding or subtracting them, depending on the operation being performed. This step involves straightforward arithmetic operations on the numerators.

4. **Simplify the resulting expression** by factoring the numerator and reducing any common factors that it shares with the denominator. This step ensures that the expression is presented in its simplest form.

Consider the example problem of adding $\frac{5}{x^2-4}$ and $\frac{2}{x-2}$.

Begin by factoring the denominators where possible. The denominator $x^2 - 4$ is a difference of squares and factors into $(x+2)(x-2)$. The expression $\dfrac{2}{x-2}$ already has $(x-2)$ as its denominator. Therefore, the LCD for these expressions is $(x+2)(x-2)$.

To adjust the second expression so that it has the LCD as its denominator, multiply both the numerator and denominator by the missing factor $(x+2)$, resulting in $\dfrac{2(x+2)}{(x+2)(x-2)}$.

Proceed to add the two expressions:

$$\frac{5}{(x+2)(x-2)} + \frac{2(x+2)}{(x+2)(x-2)} = \frac{5+2(x+2)}{(x+2)(x-2)}$$

Simplify the numerator by distributing and combining like terms:

$$\frac{5+2x+4}{(x+2)(x-2)} = \frac{2x+9}{(x+2)(x-2)}$$

Solving Equations: Isolate the Variable

To effectively address equations involving rational expressions, it is essential to adopt a meticulous and systematic methodology aimed at eliminating denominators and isolating the variable of interest. This proficiency is particularly vital for individuals preparing for the International Brotherhood of Electrical Workers (IBEW) aptitude test, which rigorously assesses one's understanding of algebraic principles and the adeptness required to manipulate complex expressions to derive accurate solutions. The primary objective is to ascertain a specific value for the variable that satisfies the conditions set forth by the equation. The inherent complexity of these expressions, characterized by the presence of variables in both the numerators and denominators, necessitates a well-defined strategy for their efficient simplification.

Commence by meticulously identifying the least common denominator (LCD) for all rational expressions present in the equation. Consider the equation $\dfrac{1}{x} + \dfrac{2}{x+2} = \dfrac{3}{x}$. In this instance, the least common denominator is determined to be the product $x(x+2)$, which encompasses all distinct factors found in the denominators of the individual rational expressions.

Once the least common denominator has been ascertained, proceed to multiply each term of the equation by this common denominator. This operation effectively eliminates the fractions by transforming each term into an equivalent expression devoid of denominators. Applying this procedure to the example equation involves multiplying each term by $x(x+2)$, thereby yielding the expression $x(x+2) \cdot \dfrac{1}{x} + x(x+2) \cdot \dfrac{2}{x+2} = x(x+2) \cdot \dfrac{3}{x}$. The simplification process entails canceling out the common factors in each term, ultimately resulting in the linear expression $x + 2 + 2x = 3(x + 2)$, which no longer contains any fractional components.

Subsequently, employ standard algebraic techniques to solve the resulting equation. This involves further simplifying the expression by distributing terms and combining like terms to effectively isolate the variable on one side of the equation. For the given example, expand the right-hand side to obtain $3x + 6 = x + 2 + 2x$. Upon further simplification, it becomes evident that the variable terms on both sides of the equation cancel each other out, revealing that the original equation is either devoid of a solution or represents an identity that holds true for all permissible values of x, provided these values do not result in division by zero in the original expression.

In scenarios where the variable can indeed be isolated, the derived solution represents the specific value that satisfies the original equation. It is imperative to rigorously verify this solution by substituting it back into the original equation to confirm its validity. This verification step ensures that the solution does not result in division by zero, which would otherwise render the solution invalid and necessitate re-evaluation of the approach taken.

Chapter 14: Inequalities & Absolute Value

14.1: Inequalities

Solving Linear Inequalities

To solve linear inequalities, the procedure involves manipulating the inequality to isolate the variable of interest, similar to solving algebraic equations. However, an additional layer of complexity is introduced due to the necessity of maintaining the correct direction of the inequality. This process fundamentally depends on the application of inverse operations, with strict adherence to sign rules, particularly when the operations involve multiplying or dividing by negative numbers.

Consider the linear inequality $3x - 5 > 7$. The primary goal is to isolate the variable x. Begin by employing the inverse operation of addition to counter the -5 on the left side of the inequality. By adding 5 to both sides, the inequality transforms into $3x > 12$. This step is critical as it eliminates the constant term on the left, simplifying the inequality. The next step involves dividing both sides by the coefficient of x, which is 3, to solve for x. This yields the inequality $x > 4$, indicating that x must be greater than 4. It is essential to note that this process mirrors that of solving an equation, with the critical distinction being the treatment of the inequality sign when multiplying or dividing by negative values.

When multiplying or dividing both sides of an inequality by a negative number, it is imperative to reverse the direction of the inequality sign. For example, consider the inequality $-2x < 6$. To isolate x, divide both sides by -2. This operation necessitates flipping the inequality sign, resulting in $x > -3$. This reversal is a fundamental rule in inequality manipulation, ensuring the solution set accurately reflects the constraints of the inequality.

Examine another example: $4 - 2x$ **7** 8. Begin by subtracting 4 from both sides, yielding $-2x$ **7** 4. The subsequent step involves dividing by -2. Remembering to reverse the inequality sign, this operation results in x **8** -2. This example underscores the importance of reversing the inequality when dividing by a negative number, a step that is often overlooked but crucial for maintaining the integrity of the inequality.

Practice Problem:
Solve the inequality $5 - 3x$ **8** $2x-10$.

1. The first step is to consolidate all terms involving x on one side of the inequality. Achieve this by adding $3x$ to both sides: 5 **8** $5x-10$. This operation effectively moves the x-terms to one side, simplifying the inequality's structure.

2. Next, isolate the *x*-terms by moving the constant terms to the opposite side. Add *10* to both sides, resulting in *15 8 5x*. This step ensures all constants are on one side, facilitating the isolation of *x*.

3. To solve for *x*, divide both sides by the coefficient of *x*, which is *5*. This yields *3 8 x*, or equivalently, *x 7 3* . This final operation isolates *x*, providing the solution to the inequality.

Strategies for Success:
- Consistently apply identical operations to both sides of the inequality to maintain equilibrium. This approach is crucial for preserving the balance of the inequality throughout the manipulation process.
- Maintain vigilance regarding the direction of the inequality, particularly when negative coefficients are present. This awareness is vital to ensure the solution accurately reflects the constraints of the inequality.
- Validate your solution by substituting a value for that should satisfy the inequality and another that should not. This verification step is a practical method to confirm the correctness of the solution.

A frequent error involves neglecting to reverse the inequality when dividing by a negative number, leading to incorrect solutions. It is imperative to meticulously double-check this step to avoid such errors, ensuring the solution's accuracy and reliability.

Graphing Solutions on Number Lines

Graphing solutions on a number line is a fundamental technique for visualizing inequalities, providing a clear and precise method to comprehend the range of values that satisfy these mathematical expressions. This graphical representation is indispensable when addressing linear inequalities such as *x > 4* or *x 7 –2*, allowing one to depict the solution set in a manner that is both intuitive and rigorous. This visualization process is particularly beneficial for candidates preparing for the International Brotherhood of Electrical Workers (IBEW) aptitude test, as it elucidates the concept of variable ranges and their direct applications in the field of electrical work, where understanding voltage, resistance, and current ranges is essential.

To accurately graph an inequality on a number line, begin by constructing a horizontal line that will serve as the baseline for plotting. This line should be marked with evenly spaced numbers to indicate potential values for the variable in question. Conventionally, zero is positioned at the center of this line, with negative integers extending to the left and positive integers extending to the right, thus providing a balanced framework for representation. For the inequality *x > 4*, identify the position of the number 4 on the number line. Given that this inequality is strict, meaning it does not include the boundary value, draw an open circle around the number 4. This open circle serves as a precise notation indicating that the number 4 itself is not part of the solution set. Subsequently, shade or draw a continuous arrow extending to the right of the number 4.

This shading or arrow visually communicates that all numbers greater than 4 are included in the solution set, effectively illustrating the infinite nature of the solutions in this direction.

For the inequality $x \geq -2$, locate the number -2 on the number line. In this case, the inequality is inclusive, signifying that the boundary value is part of the solution set. Consequently, draw a filled circle directly on the number -2 to denote its inclusion. Following this, shade or extend an arrow to the left of the number -2. This shading or arrow signifies that all numbers less than or equal to -2 are encompassed within the solution set, providing a clear visual representation of the range of values that satisfy the inequality.

When addressing compound inequalities such as $1 < x \leq 5$, the graphical representation requires a synthesis of the individual components of the inequality. Start by marking the critical values, 1 and 5, on the number line. At the position corresponding to 1, draw an open circle to signify that the value 1 is not included in the solution set. Conversely, at the position corresponding to 5, draw a filled circle to indicate that the value 5 is part of the solution set. Next, shade the segment of the number line between the open circle at 1 and the filled circle at 5. This shaded segment visually represents the continuous range of values that satisfy the compound inequality, effectively bridging the gap between the two boundary conditions.

The use of appropriate symbols—open circles for strict inequalities and filled circles for inclusive inequalities—is crucial for accurately conveying the characteristics of the solution set. This graphical method not only enhances comprehension but also serves as a powerful tool for verifying solutions obtained through algebraic methods. Mastering the skill of graphing inequalities on a number line is essential for honing the analytical abilities necessary for diagnosing and resolving issues in electrical circuits, where precise measurements and adherence to specific tolerances are often critical to ensuring proper functionality and safety.

Compound Inequalities: And/Or Cases

Compound inequalities are mathematical expressions that involve multiple conditions which must be satisfied either simultaneously or alternatively, depending on the specific requirements of the problem. These inequalities can be categorized into two primary types: "and" cases, which necessitate that both conditions are true at the same time for the solution to be valid, and "or" cases, where the validity of the solution is contingent upon at least one of the conditions being true. Mastery of solving and representing these inequalities is of paramount importance for individuals preparing for the International Brotherhood of Electrical Workers (IBEW) aptitude test, as it directly correlates with the problem-solving skills required in electrical work, where precise conditions govern the functionality and safety of circuits and systems.

In the context of "and" compound inequalities, the notation $a < x < b$ explicitly indicates that the variable x must simultaneously satisfy the condition of being greater than a and less than b. Solving these inequalities necessitates a methodical approach to isolate the variable x by applying equivalent mathematical operations on all segments of the inequality. Consider the inequality : the first step involves subtracting from each part of the inequality, yielding $-1 <$ $x < 5$. This resultant inequality defines a solution set comprising all values of x that satisfy both conditions. When graphically representing this solution on a number line, the region between -1 and 5 is shaded, with open circles placed at -1 and 5 to denote that these specific endpoints are excluded from the solution set.

Conversely, "or" compound inequalities, denoted as $x < a$ or $x > b$, convey that the variable x is required to independently fulfill either one of the conditions. The solution process involves addressing each inequality condition separately and then combining their respective solutions. Taking the example of $x < -2$ or $x > 3$, the inequalities remain in their original form, as the solutions are independent and do not require further manipulation. Graphically, this is depicted by shading the regions on the number line to the left of -2 and to the right of 3, with open circles at -2 and 3 to indicate that these endpoints are not included in the solution set.

A common pitfall in solving compound inequalities arises when the inequality sign is not reversed during the multiplication or division by a negative number, applicable to both "and" and "or" cases. For instance, when solving the inequalities $-2x > 4$ and $-3x < 9$, division by -2 and -3 respectively requires reversing the inequality signs, resulting in $x < -2$ and $x > -3$. These transformed inequalities must then be interpreted correctly within the context of whether the problem is an "and" or "or" scenario.

To develop proficiency in handling compound inequalities, it is essential to engage in consistent and focused practice. Regularly solving and graphing these inequalities will enhance one's mathematical intuition and bolster confidence in applying these concepts. It is crucial to always verify solutions by substituting back into the original inequalities to ensure they satisfy the specified conditions, thereby reinforcing accuracy and understanding.

14.2 : Absolute Value

Absolute Value as Distance from Zero

Understanding the concept of **absolute value** is a fundamental requirement for both the IBEW aptitude test and the practical aspects of electrical work. Absolute value is a mathematical function that quantifies the **magnitude of a number's distance from zero** on a one-dimensional number line, without regard to the direction of that distance. This is expressed with the notation $|x|$, where x represents any real number. The outcome of this function is always a non-negative number, reflecting the fact that distance, as a scalar quantity, inherently lacks directionality and thus cannot be negative.

To illustrate, consider the absolute value of the integer 5. The expression $|5| = 5$ signifies that the integer 5 is located precisely five units away from the origin point of zero on the number line. Conversely, for the integer -5, the notation $|-5| = 5$ conveys that -5 is similarly situated five units from zero, albeit in the negative direction. This principle is pivotal when addressing equations and inequalities that involve absolute values, as it necessitates accounting for two distinct possibilities contingent upon the sign of the variable encapsulated within the absolute value.

When solving equations that incorporate absolute values, such as $|x| = a$, where a is a positive scalar, the equation yields two potential solutions: $x = a$ and $x = -a$. This duality arises because both a and $-a$ are equidistant from zero by   units, albeit residing on opposite sides of the number line.

In the realm of practical applications, absolute values play a significant role in electrical engineering tasks, such as calculating the **net voltage difference** across a circuit. This calculation disregards the directionality of current flow, focusing solely on the magnitude of the voltage change. Mastery of this concept is indispensable for effectively diagnosing and troubleshooting electrical systems, where precision in measurement and comprehension of numerical signs are paramount for accurate analysis and resolution of electrical discrepancies.

Solving Equations & Inequalities

Mastering equations and inequalities involving absolute values necessitates a comprehensive and nuanced understanding of how these values operate within mathematical expressions. The absolute value of any given number signifies its non-negative distance from the origin point, zero, on the number line. This intrinsic property results in the existence of two potential scenarios for solutions, as absolute values inherently consider both the magnitude and direction of numbers.

Consider the specific equation $|x - 3| = 5$. Here, the expression $x - 3$ must yield a result that is precisely five units away from zero, which implies two distinct possibilities: $x - 3$ equating to either *5* or *–5*. This bifurcation arises because both *5* and *–5* are equidistant from zero on the number line. Consequently, this scenario decomposes into two separate linear equations: $x - 3 = 5$ and $x - 3 = -5$. Solving the first equation, $x - 3 = 5$, involves isolating x by adding *3* to both sides, resulting in $x = 8$. Similarly, solving the second equation, $x - 3 = -5$, requires adding *3* to both sides, yielding $x = -2$. These solutions, $x = 8$ and $x = -2$, collectively encompass all potential values of x that satisfy the original absolute value equation, ensuring that no possible solutions are overlooked.

When addressing inequalities such as $|x + 4| < 7$, the methodology necessitates a modified approach. This inequality signifies that the expression $x + 4$ must remain within a boundary of less than *7* units from zero on the number line. To express this condition algebraically, the inequality is dissected into two separate linear inequalities: $x + 4 < 7$ and $-(x + 4) < 7$. The first inequality, $x + 4 < 7$, is simplified by subtracting *4* from both sides, resulting in $x < 3$. The second inequality, $-(x + 4) < 7$, is initially rewritten as $-x - 4 < 7$. By adding *4* to both sides, we obtain

$-x < 11$, and subsequently multiplying through by -1 (which reverses the inequality sign) yields $x > -11$. Therefore, the solution set for the inequality $|x+4| < 7$ consists of all real numbers x that lie strictly between -11 and 3, explicitly excluding the endpoints -11 and 3 themselves.

A common obstacle encountered during timed assessments is the accurate application of these principles under the constraints of limited time and heightened pressure. To cultivate proficiency and enhance speed, it is imperative to engage in systematic practice with a diverse array of problems. This targeted practice fosters the development of a swift, intuitive grasp of the processes involved in solving equations and inequalities that incorporate absolute values. It is essential to meticulously consider both the positive and negative scenarios implied by absolute values, methodically working through each to ensure comprehensive coverage of all potential solutions.

Chapter 15: Functions & Graphs

15.1: Function Basics

What Is a Function?

A function serves as a fundamental concept in both mathematics and electrical engineering, delineating a precise correspondence between two distinct sets of data: inputs and outputs. This relationship is characterized by the property that each element from the input set is associated with exactly one element in the output set. This is commonly represented as $f(x) = y$, where the symbol f denotes the function itself, x represents the input variable, and y is the resulting output. Understanding this deterministic input-output relationship is essential for addressing the types of problems encountered on the IBEW aptitude test and for executing practical tasks within the realm of electrical work.

Consider a straightforward linear function: $f(x) = 2x + 3$. In this specific function, x is the independent variable, and $f(x)$ is the dependent outcome. By substituting the input value of 1 into the function, we compute the output as follows: $f(1) = 2 \times 1 + 3 = 5$. This calculation illustrates how variations in the input value x systematically alter the output y in accordance with the function's defined rule.

Functions can be presented in multiple formats, including algebraic equations, graphical plots, tabular data, or descriptive narratives. When represented graphically, the input variable is typically plotted along the horizontal axis, while the output $f(x)$ is plotted on the vertical axis. This creates a visual depiction that demonstrates how changes in the input variable affect the output value, facilitating an intuitive understanding of the relationship.

In the context of electrical work, functions are employed to model the interactions between various electrical quantities. A quintessential example is Ohm's Law, expressed as $V = IR$, which describes a function where the voltage V is a function of the current I and the resistance R. Proficiency in applying this function is indispensable for diagnosing electrical issues and for the design and analysis of electrical circuits.

To achieve proficiency in the application of functions for the IBEW aptitude test, it is imperative to focus on identifying the input and output variables, comprehending the rule that governs their relationship, and engaging in practice with a variety of representations. The skill to translate real-world situations into mathematical functions and to interpret mathematical functions in practical terms is a critical capability for effective problem-solving and informed decision-making in the electrical trade.

Function Notation and Evaluation

Function notation, expressed as *f(x)*, serves as a formal representation of the result produced by a function when a specific input, denoted by *x*, is provided. This notation is indispensable in fields such as algebra and electrical engineering, where comprehension and application of functions play a critical role in analytical problem-solving and strategic decision-making processes.

Evaluating a function involves a systematic substitution of the input value into the function's expression, followed by the execution of the mathematical operations specified within the function. Consider the function $f(x) = x^2 + 3x - 7$ as an illustrative example. When tasked with evaluating this function at a particular input, say $x = 4$, one must replace each occurrence of x in the expression with the number *4*. This substitution yields the expression $f(4) = 4^2 + 3(4) - 7$. The subsequent step involves simplifying this expression by performing the arithmetic operations in accordance with the order of operations: first, calculate the square of *4*, resulting in *16*; then, multiply *3* by *4* to obtain *12*; and finally, subtract *7* from the sum of these results. This step-by-step calculation simplifies to $f(4) = 16 + 12 - 7 = 21$. Consequently, the function evaluated at $x = 4$ produces an output of *21*, denoted as $f(4) = 21$.

Crucial concepts to grasp include:
- The notation *f(x)* succinctly represents the function's output corresponding to a specific input .
- The evaluation process necessitates substituting the designated input value for and executing the operations dictated by the function's formula.
- Proficiency in this notation is fundamental for accurately converting real-world scenarios into mathematical expressions that can be analyzed and solved.

In the domain of electrical engineering, functions serve as mathematical models that describe the interdependencies between various physical quantities. A quintessential example is Ohm's Law, articulated as *V(I) = IR*, which delineates the relationship where *V* represents the voltage across a resistor, *I* signifies the current flowing through the resistor, and *R* denotes the resistance of the resistor. Evaluating this function for a specific current value is instrumental in determining the requisite voltage to sustain that current, a task of paramount importance in the design and troubleshooting of electrical circuits.

For individuals preparing for the IBEW aptitude test, it is imperative to engage in focused practice with functions, emphasizing:
- The precise identification of input and output variables within functional relationships.
- The accurate substitution of numerical values into functional expressions, followed by meticulous calculation of the resultant output.
- The adept translation of complex word problems into function notation and the subsequent resolution of unknown variables within these mathematical representations.

15.2: Types and Graphing

Linear vs Nonlinear Patterns

Understanding the distinction between **linear** and **nonlinear** functions is crucial for accurately interpreting graphs and solving equations, particularly in the context of electrical engineering. A **linear function** is characterized by a uniform rate of change, which manifests as a straight line on a graph. The canonical form of a linear function is expressed as $y = mx + b$, where m denotes the slope, and b represents the y-intercept. The slope m quantitatively defines the steepness of the line, calculated as the ratio of the vertical change (Δy) to the horizontal change (Δx) between any two points on the line, expressed as $m = \dfrac{\Delta y}{\Delta x}$. The y-intercept b specifies the exact point at which the line intersects the y-axis, providing the value of y when x equals zero.

In contrast, **nonlinear functions** display a non-uniform rate of change, resulting in graphs that do not form straight lines. These functions encompass a variety of forms, such as quadratic functions ($y = ax^2 + bx + c$), where the presence of the x^2 term introduces a parabolic curve; exponential functions ($y = a \cdot b^x$), which exhibit exponential growth or decay depending on the base b; and trigonometric functions ($y = \sin(x), y = \cos(x)$), which produce periodic waveforms. The graphical representation of these functions reveals curves, oscillations, or other complex shapes, reflecting the variability in their rate of change.

To ascertain whether a function is linear or nonlinear, one must scrutinize specific attributes. **Linear functions** possess a *constant slope*, which is evident in their graphical representation as a straight line. Any equation that can be algebraically manipulated to conform to the structure $y = mx + b$ is inherently linear. **Nonlinear functions**, on the other hand, are characterized by variables raised to powers other than one, the presence of variables in the denominator, or operations such as squaring or taking the square root, all of which indicate a varying rate of growth or decline.

Consider the application of Ohm's Law *(V = IR)*, a pivotal concept in electrical engineering, as a practical instance. This law exemplifies a linear function where V (voltage) varies linearly with I (current) for a fixed resistance R. This linear relationship simplifies the process of performing calculations and interpreting graphs when designing and diagnosing electrical circuits, as the proportionality between voltage and current facilitates direct predictions and adjustments.

When graphing these functions, one employs a coordinate plane and systematically plots points for a range of values to discern the function's graphical representation. Linear functions yield a sequence of points that coalesce into a straight line, whereas nonlinear functions produce a trajectory that exhibits curvature, reflecting the function's changing rate of change.

Graphing with Slope and Intercepts

Graphing functions using slope and intercepts is a critical competency in both algebra and electrical engineering, serving as an indispensable tool for illustrating and analyzing the relationships between variables. The slope, symbolically represented as m, quantifies the rate of change of the dependent variable in relation to the independent variable. It is computed as the ratio of the change in the dependent variable (Δy) to the change in the independent variable (Δx) between two distinct points on the coordinate plane. Specifically, the calculation involves selecting two points on the line, noting their coordinates (x_1, y_1) and (x_2, y_2), and then applying the formula $m = \dfrac{y_2 - y_1}{x_2 - x_1}$. The y-intercept, denoted as b, is the specific coordinate on the graph where the line intersects the y-axis. This point is critical as it reveals the value of the dependent variable when the independent variable is precisely zero, providing a baseline from which the line extends.

To graph a linear equation in the standard form $y = mx + b$, the initial step involves accurately plotting the y-intercept at the coordinate *(0, b)* on the graph. This initial point is pivotal as it anchors the line, allowing the slope to dictate the line's trajectory and gradient. A positive slope m signifies an upward trajectory from left to right, indicating that as the independent variable increases, the dependent variable also increases. Conversely, a negative slope m illustrates a downward trajectory, reflecting a decrease in the dependent variable as the independent variable increases. The magnitude of the slope, represented by the absolute value $|m|$, determines the steepness of the line; greater absolute values correspond to steeper inclines or declines, while smaller values indicate a more gradual slope.

After establishing the y-intercept, the slope is employed to locate an additional point on the line, which is essential for defining the line's direction. For instance, with a slope $m = \dfrac{3}{2}$, starting from the y-intercept, one would move horizontally to the right by 2 units, corresponding to the denominator of the slope (Δx), and then vertically upward by 3 units, corresponding to the numerator (Δy). This movement identifies a second point on the line, which is subsequently marked on the graph. Connecting the y-intercept and this second point with a straight edge completes the graphical representation of the linear function.

For individuals pursuing careers as electricians, mastering the skill of graphing using slope and intercepts is invaluable beyond merely passing the IBEW aptitude test. It lays a crucial groundwork for interpreting electrical properties graphically. A pertinent example is Ohm's Law, expressed as $V = IR$, which can be graphed as a linear equation where the current *(I)* functions as the independent variable, the voltage *(V)* as the dependent variable, and the resistance *(R)* as the slope of the line. In this scenario, the graph features no y-intercept because the line originates from the origin, indicating zero voltage when there is no current. This graphical depiction is instrumental in visualizing how variations in current influence the voltage across a resistor, which is a fundamental concept in the analysis and understanding of electrical circuits.

Real-World Models

Aspiring electricians acquire a comprehensive understanding of practical applications by engaging with real-world mathematical models through the detailed study of functions and graphs, which facilitates the direct application of abstract mathematical concepts to tangible electrical tasks. This methodical approach significantly enhances their capacity to tackle complex problems and deepens their practical knowledge base. Within the domain of electrical engineering, functions serve as precise mathematical representations that describe the intricate relationships between various electrical quantities, such as voltage *(V)*, current *(I)*, and resistance *(R)*. Mastering these relationships empowers individuals to accurately predict and manipulate electrical behaviors, thereby ensuring both the safety and efficiency of electrical systems.

Consider the intricate process of designing a lighting circuit for a newly constructed building. The electrician must meticulously calculate the total resistance of the circuit to determine the appropriate wire gauge, ensuring that it can safely accommodate the anticipated electrical load. Ohm's Law, expressed as $V = IR$, where V denotes voltage, I denotes current, and R denotes resistance, models this specific scenario. By algebraically rearranging this equation to solve for resistance, $R = \dfrac{V}{I}$, the electrician can accurately compute the necessary resistance based on the known voltage supplied by the power source and the specific current requirements of the lighting fixtures. This calculation is critical for ensuring that the selected wire gauge can handle the current without overheating, which could lead to circuit failure or safety hazards.

The role of functions extends further into the realm of power consumption analysis. The power *(P)* consumed by an electrical device is directly dependent on both the voltage *(V)* and the current *(I)*, as articulated by the equation $P = VI$. This mathematical relationship is instrumental in enabling electricians to compute the power consumption of devices, which is crucial for designing circuits that are not only efficient but also adhere to safety standards. By knowing the circuit's voltage and the power rating of a device, an electrician can determine the current that the device will draw. This information is vital for selecting the appropriate circuit breakers and wiring, which are essential components in preventing circuit overloading and mitigating the risk of fire hazards.

Graphs of these functions provide a visual representation that significantly aids electricians in comprehending how variations in one variable influence another. For instance, a graph illustrating Ohm's Law demonstrates a linear relationship between voltage and current, indicating that, assuming resistance remains constant, an increase in voltage results in a proportional increase in current. This visual tool is invaluable for electricians as it allows them to predict how modifications to the circuit, such as the addition of more resistance, will affect overall circuit performance. Understanding these graphical relationships equips electricians with the ability to make informed decisions about circuit design and troubleshooting, ensuring optimal functionality and safety.

Chapter 16: Function Information Analysis

16.1: Graph Interpretation

Domain & Range

Understanding the domain and range of a function is essential for electricians and apprentices, as it establishes the foundation for analyzing and interpreting the behavior of electrical systems through graphical representations. The domain encompasses all permissible input values, analogous to the various levels of voltage or resistance applicable within a circuit. Conversely, the range includes all resultant output values, akin to the current flow or power output generated under those specified conditions.

To accurately ascertain the domain, one must examine the function in question and consider, "What input values can be utilized without inducing any mathematical anomalies or errors?" In the scenario of Ohm's Law, expressed as $V = IR$, the domain comprises all real numbers since any conceivable voltage *(V)* or resistance *(R)* value can theoretically be applied without resulting in mathematical inconsistencies. Nonetheless, practical constraints, such as the maximum voltage a material can endure before breakdown occurs, may impose limitations on the domain in real-world scenarios. For instance, if a circuit material has a dielectric breakdown voltage of 300 volts, the domain would then be restricted to input values resulting in voltages below this threshold to prevent circuit failure.

The range is determined by evaluating the function over its domain and identifying the resultant output values. Taking Ohm's Law as an example, if resistance *(R)* is held constant, the range of possible current *(I)* values is directly proportional to the applied voltage. As the voltage increases, the current increases linearly, provided that resistance remains unchanged. This relationship is linear, and the theoretical range includes all real numbers. However, physical limitations, such as the maximum current a conductor can safely carry without overheating, impose practical constraints on the range. For example, a wire with a current-carrying capacity of 10 amperes would limit the range to currents below this value to avoid overheating and potential damage.

To graphically determine the domain and range, one can plot the function on a Cartesian coordinate system. The horizontal axis, or x-axis, represents the domain, while the vertical axis, or y-axis, represents the range. For linear functions, such as $y = mx + b$, where *m* denotes the slope and *b* signifies the y-intercept, the line extends infinitely in both the positive and negative directions, indicating a domain and range that encompass all real numbers. However, for a function like $y = \sqrt{x}$, the domain is restricted to $x \geq 0$ because the square root of a negative number results in complex numbers, which are not applicable in basic electrical engineering contexts. The range for this function is similarly limited to $y \geq 0$, as the square root of any non-negative real number yields a positive or zero result, reflecting the non-negative nature of the square root operation.

Key Graph Features

Key graph features such as slope, intercepts, and turning points are integral to the intricate analysis of function behavior, closely aligning with the foundational concepts in electrical engineering, including Ohm's Law and power consumption dynamics. The slope of a graph, denoted as m in the linear equation $y = mx + b$, quantifies the rate at which the dependent variable, often current (I) in electrical contexts, changes with respect to the independent variable, typically voltage (V). A steep slope, characterized by a large absolute value of $|m|$, signifies a rapid variation in the dependent variable. This scenario is commonly observed in circuits where a small increment in voltage results in a substantial increase in current, provided that resistance (R) remains unchanged, exemplifying a low-resistance path. In contrast, a shallow slope, where $|m|$ is small, indicates a gradual change, reflecting a circuit with significant resistance that impedes the flow of current.

The y-intercept, represented by b, identifies the coordinate where the graph intersects the y-axis, specifically when $x = 0$. This feature is pivotal for interpreting initial conditions, such as the baseline current in a circuit prior to the application of any voltage. Within the framework of Ohm's Law, a graph exhibiting a y-intercept at zero $(b = 0)$ implies that no current flows in the absence of an applied voltage, a scenario consistent with the fundamental principles governing electrical circuits, where current is directly proportional to voltage when resistance is constant.

Turning points on a graph delineate the locations where the function experiences a change in direction, transitioning from an increasing to a decreasing trend or vice versa. These critical points are particularly significant in the analysis of non-linear functions, such as those modeling alternating current (AC) circuits or the charge and discharge cycles of capacitors. Identifying these turning points is essential for predicting the extremum values of variables such as current and voltage, ensuring that they remain within the safe operational thresholds of electrical components, thus preventing potential damage due to overloading or underutilization.

Increasing/Decreasing Intervals

Understanding the intricacies of increasing and decreasing intervals on a graph is critical for comprehending the dynamic interactions between variables within electrical systems. These intervals provide insight into where a function exhibits growth or decline as one progresses from left to right along the x-axis. This understanding is particularly important when analyzing the behavior of electrical currents and voltages in response to variations in resistance or other influencing factors within the system.

An increasing interval is characterized by a scenario in which the output, represented by the y-value, experiences growth as the input, represented by the x-value, rises. Consider the scenario where the voltage applied across a resistor is incrementally increased. This action results in an elevated current flow through the resistor. By graphically representing the current *(I)* on the y-axis and the voltage *(V)* on the x-axis, and utilizing Ohm's Law $(I = \frac{V}{R})$, one can observe an increasing interval on the graph. This is contingent upon the resistance *(R)* remaining constant, as the current exhibits a direct proportionality to the voltage, resulting in a linear increase.

Conversely, a decreasing interval is observed when the output diminishes as the input increases. This phenomenon occurs in systems where an increase in one variable precipitates a decrease in another due to inverse relationships. For example, in a circuit powered by a fixed power supply, an increase in resistance leads to a reduction in current flow. This relationship can be quantified using the formula $P = IV$, where *P* denotes power. If the power *(P)* is held constant and the resistance *(R)* is increased, the current *(I)* must decrease to maintain the equation's balance. This scenario manifests as a decreasing interval on a graph plotting current *(I)* against resistance *(R)*.

To accurately identify these intervals, one must scrutinize the graph for sections where the curve ascends, indicating an increasing interval, or descends, indicating a decreasing interval, as one traces the graph from left to right. The slope of the tangent line at any given point on the curve serves as a precise indicator of the rate at which the function is increasing or decreasing at that specific point. A positive slope signifies an increasing interval, while a negative slope denotes a decreasing interval.

For electricians and apprentices, honing the ability to discern and analyze these intervals is imperative to anticipate how modifications in one component of a circuit will affect the entire system. This skill is essential for effective troubleshooting and optimization of circuit performance, ensuring that electrical installations operate safely and efficiently.

16.2 : Representation & Translation

Tables & Graphs

Electricians must possess a comprehensive understanding of how to interpret data meticulously extracted from function tables and graphs, as this proficiency translates intricate electrical principles into clear visual representations. Function tables serve as a systematic framework for organizing input-output relationships, where each distinct input variable, such as voltage *(V)* or resistance *(R)*, corresponds precisely to a specific output variable, like current

(1). To interpret these tables accurately, electricians should concentrate on discerning the pattern of variation between inputs and outputs. For instance, if both the input and output values double in magnitude, this suggests a linear relationship, indicative of direct proportionality, as exemplified by Ohm's Law *(V = RI)*, where the ratio of voltage to current remains constant, reflecting a fixed resistance.

Graphs provide a visual illustration of these relationships, with input variables systematically plotted along the horizontal x-axis and output variables along the vertical y-axis. The slope *(m)* of a line is a crucial parameter, representing the rate of change of the output relative to the input. A steep slope indicates a rapid change, which can be interpreted as low electrical resistance in the circuit, allowing for a significant increase in current with a minor increase in voltage. Conversely, a shallow slope signifies high resistance, where substantial increases in voltage result in minimal changes in current. The y-intercept *(b)* is another critical feature, revealing the output value when the input is zero, which could denote the initial current present in a circuit prior to the application of any external voltage, providing insight into inherent circuit characteristics.

To transition data from tables to graphs, it is essential to accurately plot each input-output pair from the table onto the graph. The formation of a straight line by these points strongly indicates a linear relationship. However, if the plotted points form a curve, this signifies a nonlinear relationship, necessitating further analysis to ascertain the specific nature of the relationship, which could be quadratic, where the change in output is proportional to the square of the input, or exponential, where the rate of change of the output increases exponentially with the input.

When analyzing graphs, it is imperative to focus on critical features such as intercepts, which provide valuable insights into initial conditions, and the slope, which illustrates the rate at which conditions evolve. Electricians must thoroughly comprehend these concepts to diagnose and troubleshoot electrical systems effectively, enabling them to anticipate system behavior under various operational conditions, thereby ensuring optimal performance and safety.

Translating Forms

Electricians must develop a proficiency in the intricate process of translating mathematical equations into graphical representations, and vice versa, to effectively bridge the gap between theoretical concepts and their practical applications. This entails the transformation of algebraic expressions into visual data forms and converting visual data back into algebraic expressions, a fundamental competence necessary for the interpretation of electrical systems and the efficient resolution of complex technical challenges.

Consider the linear equation $y = mx + b$, where m represents the slope of the line, quantifying the rate of change in the dependent variable y with respect to the independent variable x, and b denotes the y-intercept, which indicates the specific point at which the line intersects the y-a is. In the domain of electrical work, this equation can be analogous to the relationship between voltage *(V)* and current *(I)* as defined by Ohm's Law, expressed as $V = IR$, where R signifies resistance. Constructing a graph of this equation enables the visualization of the effect of variations in voltage on current, assuming resistance remains constant.

To accurately graph this equation, one begins by identifying and plotting the y-intercept (*b*) on the y-axis. Subsequently, the slope (*m*), which may represent the resistance in an electrical circuit, is employed to calculate the 'rise over run' — the change in current (*I*) relative to a given change in voltage (*V*). By systematically plotting multiple points corresponding to different voltage values and drawing a straight line through these points, the linear relationship between voltage and current is elucidated, thereby illustrating the direct proportionality dictated by Ohm's Law.

The process of converting a graph back into an equation involves the precise determination of the slope and y-intercept from the graphical representation. For instance, if a graph depicts a line that intersects the y-axis at *2* (indicating the y-intercept, *b*) and exhibits a slope (*m*) of *3*, signifying that for each unit increase in *x*, *y* increases by *3*, the corresponding equation would be $y = 3x + 2$. This equation can be utilized to compute specific values or to make predictions in electrical contexts, such as calculating the necessary voltage to achieve a desired current level.

Electricians who master these conversion techniques can effectively visualize intricate electrical relationships and execute precise calculations. This capability is vital for success on the IBEW aptitude test and for practical problem-solving in the field, where depicting electrical circuits as graphical models facilitates troubleshooting and enhances the efficiency of designing and analyzing electrical systems.

Chapter 17: Number & Pattern Series

17.1: Recognizing Sequences

Arithmetic Sequences

Arithmetic sequences represent a critical area of study within the mathematical domain, defined by an ordered set of numbers where each successive term is derived by the addition of a fixed, unchanging value, referred to as the common difference. This common difference, denoted by d, can assume positive, negative, or zero values, thereby producing sequences that exhibit increasing, decreasing, or constant behavior, respectively. The ability to identify and analyze these sequences is essential for addressing a variety of mathematical challenges, particularly those involving pattern recognition and series computation, as frequently encountered in the International Brotherhood of Electrical Workers (IBEW) aptitude assessments.

To accurately determine whether a sequence of numbers is arithmetic, one must calculate the difference between each pair of successive terms in the sequence with care. If this calculated difference remains consistent throughout the entire sequence, then the sequence can be classified as arithmetic. The formula used to compute the nth term of an arithmetic sequence is expressed as $a_n = a_1 + (n-1)d$, where a_n represents the term at position n, a_1 is the initial term of the sequence, signifies the position index of the term within the sequence, and d is the common difference. This formula provides a method for directly calculating any term within the sequence without requiring the enumeration of all preceding terms, thereby enhancing the efficiency of problem-solving processes.

To continue an arithmetic sequence beyond the given terms, one must systematically apply the common difference to the most recent term. For example, if a sequence begins with a known set of terms, the subsequent term is determined by adding the common difference to the last term of the known set. This procedure can be repeated iteratively to generate any required number of terms or to locate a specific term deep within the sequence.

For instance, consider an arithmetic sequence where the initial term $a_1 = 3$ and the common difference $d = 4$. To determine the value of the 5th term in this sequence, one would utilize the formula: $a_5 = 3 + (5-1) \times 4 = 3 + 16 = 19$. This systematic approach not only facilitates the extension of sequences but also proves invaluable in resolving complex mathematical problems where understanding the interdependence of terms is crucial.

Geometric Sequences

Geometric sequences are distinct from arithmetic sequences due to their evolution through a process of multiplication or division by a constant factor, referred to as the common ratio (r).

This characteristic enables each subsequent term to be generated by multiplying the previous term by r, thereby resulting in patterns of exponential growth or decay. For individuals training to become electricians, understanding geometric sequences is crucial, as they frequently underpin the calculations involved in analyzing electrical phenomena that exhibit exponential variation. Such phenomena include alternating current waveforms, which can be described using sinusoidal functions that inherently involve geometric progression, as well as the charging and discharging cycles of capacitors in resistor-capacitor (RC) circuits, where the voltage across the capacitor changes exponentially over time.

To ascertain whether a sequence is geometric, it is essential to verify that the ratio between consecutive terms remains constant. This is accomplished by dividing any term in the sequence by the term immediately preceding it. If the resulting ratio (r) is uniform throughout the sequence, then the sequence is classified as geometric. The mathematical expression for the nth term of a geometric sequence is given by $a_n = a_1 \cdot r^{(n-1)}$, where a_n denotes the term located at position n, a_1 signifies the first term, and n represents the position of the term within the sequence. This formula facilitates the direct computation of any specific term in the sequence without the necessity to calculate all preceding terms, thereby streamlining the process of sequence analysis.

Consider a practical application in an electrical circuit characterized by a pulsating voltage that doubles at each discrete time interval. Suppose the initial voltage (a_1) is 2 volts, and the common ratio (r) is 2. To determine the voltage after 3 intervals ($n = 4$), one can apply the formula: $a_4 = 2 \cdot 2^{(4-1)} = 2 \cdot 2^3 = 16$ volts. This example illustrates how geometric sequences can effectively model real-world electrical behaviors, providing electricians with the capability to forecast outcomes over time or across various components within a circuit.

The aspect of decay in geometric sequences, where the common ratio satisfies $0 < r < 1$, holds significant importance. This scenario is commonly encountered in electrical circuits where resistance leads to a reduction in current or voltage over time. For instance, when a capacitor discharges through a resistor, it may experience a halving of its voltage at each time interval.

This behavior is represented by a geometric sequence with a common ratio of $r = \dfrac{1}{2}$, capturing

the exponential decrease in voltage as the capacitor releases its stored energy through the resistive element.

17.2: Rules and Challenges

Finding the Next Term

To predict the subsequent term in a numerical sequence, a methodical approach that integrates keen observation with rigorous mathematical principles is indispensable. The initial step involves meticulously identifying the underlying pattern that governs the sequence's progression. This pattern may manifest as a straightforward arithmetic progression, character-ized by each term increasing or decreasing by a uniform numerical increment, known as the common difference. Alternatively, the pattern could be a geometric progression, where each term is derived by multiplying or dividing the preceding term by a constant factor, referred to as the common ratio. Sequences may also adhere to more intricate rules, which could include alternating patterns, recursive relationships, or formula-based progressions, necessitating a profound comprehension of advanced mathematical concepts to decipher their structure.

In the realm of arithmetic sequences, the task of determining the next term hinges on accu-rately identifying the common difference, denoted as . Once this value is ascertained, the sub-sequent term ($a_n + 1$) is calculated by adding d to the most recent term in the sequence (a_n). The mathematical expression $a_{n+1} = a_n + d$ encapsulates this process. For instance, consider a sce-nario where $d = 3$ and the current term is 12; the forthcoming term is computed as $12 + 3 = 15$.

In contrast, geometric sequences fundamentally rely on the common ratio, symbolized by r. The procedure to ascertain the next term involves multiplying the latest term by this ratio, as articulated in the formula $a_{n+1} = a_n \cdot r$. For example, if a sequence progresses through the mech-anism of doubling each term and the present term is 6, the ensuing term is determined by the calculation $6 \cdot 2 = 12$.

Certain sequences adhere to patterns predicated on more sophisticated mathematical func-tions or rules. For example, a sequence might be structured around the squares of natural numbers or incorporate alternating mathematical operations. A critical step involves com-prehending the foundational rule, such as recognizing that terms are generated by applying a particular mathematical operation to the term's position within the sequence, exemplified by $a_n = n^2$ for sequences involving squares of natural numbers.

When addressing sequences that integrate alternating patterns or recursive relationships, the strategy for predicting the subsequent term must be adapted accordingly. Alternating sequenc-es may oscillate between two or more distinct rules, necessitating meticulous observation to ascertain which rule governs the impending term. Recursive sequences, wherein each term is defined based on one or more preceding terms, demand the calculation of intermediate terms to extrapolate the next term.

Writing Rules for Algebraic Sequences

To express sequences algebraically, it is essential to thoroughly analyze and comprehend the intrinsic pattern governing the sequence. This understanding facilitates the development of a mathematical formula that enables the prediction of any term within the sequence without the need to enumerate each individual term. Within the context of electrical studies and the IBEW aptitude test, practitioners frequently encounter two predominant types of sequences: arithmetic sequences and geometric sequences. Each of these types possesses a distinct meth-odology for algebraic representation.

Arithmetic Sequences: In arithmetic sequences, each subsequent term is derived by adding a constant value, referred to as the common difference d, to the preceding term. The mathematical expression for the nth term of an arithmetic sequence is represented by the formula $a_n = a_1 + (n-1)d$. Here, a_1 denotes the initial term of the sequence, and n signifies the position of the term within the sequence. To illustrate, consider a sequence where the first term $a_1 = 5$ and the common difference $d = 3$. To calculate the third term ($n = 3$), substitute the known values into the formula: $a_3 = 5 + (3-1) \times 3$. This calculation simplifies to $a_3 = 5 + 2 \times 3 = 5 + 6 = 11$.

Geometric Sequences: Geometric sequences are characterized by each term being produced through multiplication or division by a constant ratio, denoted as r, relative to the preceding term. The formula for determining the nth term of a geometric sequence is expressed as $a_n = a_1 \cdot r^{(n-1)}$. For example, if the initial term of the sequence is $a_1 = 2$ and the common ratio is $r = 2$, the fourth term can be calculated by substituting these values into the formula: $a_4 = 2 \cdot 2^{(4-1)}$. This computation results in $a_4 = 2 \cdot 2^3 = 2 \cdot 8 = 16$.

To effectively construct algebraic expressions for sequences, adhere to the following procedural steps:

1. **Identify the Type:** Initiate the process by discerning whether the sequence in question is arithmetic or geometric. This determination involves scrutinizing the sequence's pattern of progression to ascertain whether it entails a constant additive difference or a multiplicative ratio.

2. **Determine the Constants:** For arithmetic sequences, it is essential to ascertain the common difference (d), which is the fixed amount added to each term to yield the subsequent term. For geometric sequences, identify the common ratio (r), which is the factor by which each term is multiplied to produce the next term.

3. **Apply the Formula:** Employ the appropriate algebraic formula based on the type of sequence. Substitute the identified values of a_1, d or r, and n into the formula to compute the desired nth term with precision.

For sequences that do not conform neatly to the arithmetic or geometric categories, such as those involving alternating patterns or more intricate functions, it is necessary to devise a function that encapsulates the sequence's behavior. For instance, if a sequence alternates between adding 2 and multiplying by -1, it may be requisite to employ piecewise functions that delineate each step contingent on the term's position (n).

Visual Patterns

Visual patterns present a unique set of challenges, necessitating solvers to meticulously identify and analyze the intricate relationships between various attributes such as shapes, spatial positions, and, occasionally, color hues or dimensional sizes. Unlike numerical sequences, which can often be resolved through the application of specific mathematical formulas or algorithms, visual patterns require a more nuanced and intuitive approach. This approach involves advanced spatial reasoning skills and the capacity to detect and interpret subtle variations or consistencies that manifest across a series of images or diagrams.

To adeptly address visual patterns, one must focus on critical elements, including the precise number of objects, their orientation, geometric shape, and their positional arrangement relative to one another within the pattern. For instance, consider a pattern comprising a sequence of geometric shapes where each subsequent shape features an additional side compared to its predecessor. Identifying this pattern necessitates a careful count of the sides of each shape, followed by a detailed observation of the incremental addition of sides as the sequence progresses.

Visual patterns frequently incorporate transformations such as rotation, reflection, or scaling. For example, a square might undergo a 90-degree clockwise rotation with each successive step in the sequence. Detecting this pattern requires keen observation of both the rotational direction and the precise angle of rotation consistently applied throughout the entire sequence.

Examine a pattern where a triangle initially points upwards, is succeeded by a square, and then followed by a triangle pointing downwards, repeating in this specific sequence. This pattern encompasses both a transformation in shape and an alteration in orientation. To accurately predict the subsequent figure in the sequence, one must meticulously observe the established sequence and apply the deduced rules: following a triangle pointing downwards, the pattern recommences with a triangle oriented upwards.

When faced with a complex visual pattern, it is essential to deconstruct it into more manageable components. Consider posing the following analytical questions:

- Is there a discernible repetitive sequence in the shapes or figures presented?
- Do the objects exhibit a systematic increase or decrease in size?
- Is there a consistent alteration in color or shading applied throughout the sequence?
- How do the objects transition or rotate from one step to the subsequent one?

Engaging in regular practice with a diverse array of visual patterns is vital. Start with straightforward sequences and progressively tackle more complex ones. Utilize graph paper to meticulously sketch sequences, documenting changes at each step with precision. This tactile approach reinforces spatial reasoning skills, which are crucial for achieving proficiency in deciphering visual patterns.

Chapter 18: Probability & Statistics

18.1 : Core Concepts

Probability Basics

Understanding the foundational principles of probability is essential for individuals preparing for the IBEW aptitude test, given its significant role in various electrical scenarios and complex problem-solving tasks. Probability is the mathematical study of the likelihood that a particular event will occur within a specified set of possible outcomes. This likelihood is expressed as a numerical value ranging from 0 to 1, where 0 represents an event that is impossible and 1 denotes an event that is certain to occur.

To determine the probability P of a specific event E occurring within a finite sample space S, one must apply the formula $P(E) = \dfrac{Number\ of\ outcomes\ favorable\ to\ E}{Total\ number\ of\ outcomes\ in\ S}$. For instance, consider the scenario of flipping a fair coin. The probability of the coin landing heads up ($P(H)$) is calculated as $\dfrac{1}{2}$. This is because there is precisely one favorable outcome (the coin showing heads) out of a total of two possible outcomes (either heads or tails).

In the context of electrical work, probability is utilized to evaluate the likelihood of various system failures, to determine the reliability of individual components, and to predict the outcomes of different circuit configurations under fluctuating conditions. This foundational understanding of probability empowers aspiring electricians to make informed decisions and accurate predictions within their professional field.

Probability events are categorized into three primary types: simple events, compound events, and mutually exclusive events. A simple event refers to an event with only a single outcome, such as the act of drawing a red card from a standard deck of cards. A compound event, on the other hand, involves the occurrence of two or more simple events simultaneously, such as drawing a card that is both red and a king. Mutually exclusive events are those that cannot occur at the same time, exemplified by the impossibility of drawing a card that is simultaneously a heart and a club from a single deck.

Essential formulas in probability include the addition rule for mutually exclusive events, expressed as *P(A or B) = P(A) + P(B)*, and the multiplication rule for independent events, given by *P(A and B) = P(A) × P(B)*. These mathematical rules are indispensable when addressing complex scenarios that involve multiple potential outcomes or when evaluating the probability of sequential events occurring in a given sequence.

Theoretical vs Experimental Data

Understanding the distinction between theoretical and experimental probability is crucial for those preparing for the IBEW aptitude test, particularly aspiring electricians who must navigate complex electrical systems. Theoretical probability is mathematically defined as

$$P(E) = \frac{Number \quad of \quad favorable \quad outcomes}{Total \quad number \quad of \quad outcomes}$$. This definition presupposes a perfectly uniform sample

space wherein each outcome possesses an identical likelihood of occurrence. For example, when considering the simple act of flipping a fair coin, the theoretical probability of the coin

landing on heads is calculated as $\frac{1}{2}$. This value is derived from the fact that the sample space

consists of two equally probable outcomes: heads and tails, each with a probability of *0.5*, assuming no external forces influence the coin's behavior.

In contrast, experimental probability is derived from empirical data obtained through the execu-

tion of actual experiments. It is computed using the formula $P(E) = \frac{Number \quad of \quad times \quad event \quad occurs}{Total \quad number \quad of \quad trials}$.

For instance, if an experiment involves flipping a coin 100 times and observing that it lands

on heads *55* times, the experimental probability of obtaining heads is $\frac{55}{100} = 0.55$. This observed

value may deviate from the theoretical probability due to the inherent randomness present in real-world experiments or due to unaccounted variables that might not be included in the theoretical model, such as minor biases in the coin or variations in the flipping technique.

The primary distinction between theoretical and experimental probability lies in their respective methodologies and applications. Theoretical probability serves as a foundational tool for predicting the likelihood of events in a controlled, idealized environment. This is particularly beneficial for electricians who need to anticipate the behavior of electrical systems under standardized conditions, enabling them to understand potential outcomes without the interference of external factors. Conversely, experimental probability provides valuable insights into the operation of systems in real-world scenarios, where conditions are frequently far from ideal. This approach allows electricians to refine their expectations and calculations based on observed performance data, thereby enhancing the accuracy and reliability of system designs and troubleshooting efforts by accounting for real-world variables and anomalies.

18.2: Working with Data

Mean, Median, Mode, Range

Understanding the intricacies of statistical measures such as the mean, median, mode, and range is essential for conducting precise data analysis, which is integral to both the International Brotherhood of Electrical Workers (IBEW) aptitude assessments and the daily operations of electrical work. These statistical instruments provide a comprehensive examination of data distribution, thereby facilitating the process of making informed decisions.

The mean, commonly referred to as the arithmetic average, is calculated by summing all numerical values within a data set and subsequently dividing this sum by the count of the numbers present. For instance, consider a set of electrical current measurements: 2 amperes (A), 3A, 4A, and 5A. To compute the mean current, one adds these values, yielding a total of 14A. This total is then divided by the number of measurements, which in this case is four, resulting in a mean current value of 3.5A. This measure provides insight into the central tendency of the data set, indicating the average current level.

The median is the value that separates the higher half from the lower half of a data set once it has been organized in non-decreasing order. In instances where the data set contains an even number of observations, the median is determined by calculating the mean of the two central numbers. For example, given the data set 2, 4, 7, 12, the data is already in ascending order. The two middle numbers are 4 and 7, and their average, calculated as $\frac{4+7}{2}$, yields a median of 5.5.

This measure highlights the central point of the data distribution, providing a robust indicator of the data's midpoint that is less susceptible to outliers compared to the mean.

The mode is defined as the value or values that appear with the highest frequency within a data set. It is possible for a data set to be unimodal, bimodal, or multimodal if one, two, or more values, respectively, occur with equal highest frequency. For example, in the data set 1, 2, 2, 3, 4, 4, both the values 2 and 4 appear twice, more frequently than any other numbers, rendering the set bimodal with modes at 2 and 4. The mode is particularly useful for understanding the most common value or values in a data set, which can be critical in identifying prevalent trends or patterns.

The range is a measure of dispersion that quantifies the extent of variation in a data set by subtracting the smallest value from the largest value. For instance, in the data set 3, 7, 8, 15, the range is calculated by subtracting the minimum value, 3, from the maximum value, 15, resulting in a range of 12. This measure provides a straightforward indication of the spread of the data, offering insights into the variability present within the data set.

Charts & Graphs Interpretation

Interpreting charts and graphs is an essential skill for analyzing data within the framework of the IBEW aptitude test and the broader electrical field. These visual representations transform intricate datasets into digestible and actionable insights. It is crucial to discern the specific type of graph being utilized, as each visualization format serves a distinct analytical purpose. Line graphs, for instance, are proficient at tracking temporal changes, making them particularly beneficial for identifying trends or comparing variations across multiple groups over a defined period. The x-axis of a line graph typically denotes time intervals, such as days, months, or years, while the y-axis represents the quantitative measure being tracked, such as voltage levels, current flow, or energy consumption. Bar graphs, in contrast, are optimized for juxtaposing quantities across varying categories. Here, the x-axis might represent different categories such as types of electrical components, while the y-axis signifies the numerical value, such as efficiency ratings or failure rates. Pie charts, by contrast, are designed to illustrate percentage or proportional data of a whole entity, where each slice corresponds to a fraction of the total dataset, often depicted in terms of market share, resource allocation, or component distribution.

To proficiently interpret these graphical representations, begin by scrutinizing the title to gain contextual understanding. This step provides an initial framework regarding the dataset, such as the scope, timeframe, and specific variables involved. Next, direct your attention to the axes in bar or line graphs: the x-axis (horizontal) generally represents the categories or chronological intervals, while the y-axis (vertical) indicates the measured values, which could range from kilowatt-hours to amperage. For pie charts, it is imperative to identify the legend, which deciphers each segment, often color-coded, to its corresponding category or variable. Careful attention should be given to the scale employed; a graph may utilize a compressed scale to accentuate differences or an expanded scale to downplay them, thus influencing the perceived significance of the data.

Examine the data to uncover trends, discern patterns, or detect outliers. In the context of a line graph, an upward trajectory signifies an increase over time, such as a rise in electrical demand, while a downward trajectory denotes a decrease, potentially indicating reduced energy consumption or efficiency gains. For bar graphs, the comparative analysis of bar lengths allows for the determination of the largest or smallest categories, such as the most prevalent type of electrical fault or the most efficient energy source. In pie charts, larger segments visually represent a greater proportion of the whole, such as a dominant market leader or a primary resource consumer.

Contemplate the implications of these observed trends and patterns. For example, a sustained increase in electrical consumption over several months, as depicted on a line graph, could signify an escalating demand that necessitates strategic planning and resource allocation. Similarly, a bar graph that contrasts the efficiency of various types of electrical systems can facilitate the identification of the most effective option, thereby guiding decision-making processes in system design or energy management.

Engage in the interpretation of charts and graphs with a discerning and analytical mindset. Consider what the data may not reveal, such as external variables influencing the outcomes or data that has been excluded from the analysis. Recognizing the constraints and limitations of the presented data is essential in preventing misinterpretations and ensuring a more precise and comprehensive analysis.

Word Problems in Stats and Probability

Addressing real-world challenges in statistics and probability necessitates a systematic and rigorous approach that integrates theoretical frameworks with practical applications. For instance, an electrical company aiming to ascertain the probability of system failures occurring within a designated temporal window must employ a combination of probability theory and statistical analysis to refine its maintenance schedules and optimize the allocation of resources. This entails a precise and detailed process.

Initially, the process begins with defining the sample space, which is the comprehensive set of all conceivable outcomes related to system failures over the specified duration. This requires a thorough examination of historical data, which may indicate that the system encounters an average of 5 failures per month. Such historical insights facilitate the modeling of the probability of observing a specified number of failures using the Poisson distribution. The Poisson distribution is mathematically expressed by the formula:

$$P(X = k) = \frac{\lambda^k e^{-\lambda}}{k!}$$

In this formula, $P(X = k)$ denotes the probability of exactly k failures occurring within the given timeframe. The parameter λ represents the average rate of occurrences, which in this scenario is 5 failures per month. The constant e refers to the base of the natural logarithm, approximately valued at 2.71828, which is crucial for calculating probabilities in continuous growth processes.

To compute the probability of precisely 3 failures occurring in one month, we substitute $k = 3$ and $\lambda = 5$ into the Poisson probability formula:

$$P(X = 3) = \frac{5^3 e^{-5}}{3!} = \frac{125 \times e^{-5}}{6} \approx 0.1404$$

This computation indicates that there is a 14.04% probability of exactly 3 failures occurring within a month, thereby providing a quantifiable measure of risk for the company.

Moreover, the company may require an understanding of the variability in the monthly number of failures. This necessitates the calculation of both the variance and standard deviation of the Poisson distribution. For a Poisson distribution, the variance (σ^2) is equivalent to the mean (λ), thus making it 5. The standard deviation (σ) is derived by taking the square root of the variance:

$$\sigma = \sqrt{\sigma^2} = \sqrt{5} \approx 2.236$$

This standard deviation implies that the typical deviation from the mean number of failures (5) is approximately 2.236 in any given month, offering insights into the expected fluctuation range.

These statistical tools empower the electrical company to predict and prepare for various potential outcomes regarding system failures. By leveraging these probability and statistical methodologies, the company can make strategic decisions related to workforce allocation, scheduling of preventive maintenance activities, and deployment of resources in a manner that minimizes operational downtime and enhances the reliability of service delivery.

Chapter 19: Geometry Essentials

19.1: Shapes and Properties

Lines and Angles

Understanding the foundational concepts of lines and angles is crucial in the field of geometry, as these elements form the basis for more complex geometric theories and applications. In the realm of geometry, a line is defined as an abstract concept that possesses no thickness or width, extending infinitely in both directions. This infinite extension is represented by a straight path with arrows at both ends, symbolizing its endless nature. Lines serve as the primary building blocks for defining shapes and figures, and their properties are pivotal in formulating geometric postulates and theorems.

Angles are formed when two rays or line segments converge at a single point, referred to as the vertex. The measurement of an angle is determined by the degree of rotation required to align one ray with the other, using the vertex as the pivot point. This measurement is expressed in degrees, a unit that quantifies the size of the angle based on a circle divided into 360 equal parts.

The classification of angles is based on the specific range of their measurements:

- **Acute angles** are those whose measurements are strictly less than 90°. These angles are frequently encountered in various geometric constructions and are characterized by their sharp appearance.

- **Right angles** are precisely 90° and are fundamental in defining perpendicularity. The presence of a right angle is denoted by a small square placed at the vertex, indicating the perfect quarter-turn rotation between the rays.

- **Obtuse angles** have measurements that exceed 90° but remain below 180°. These angles appear more open than acute angles and are crucial in the study of polygons and other geometric shapes.

- **Straight angles** are exactly 180°, representing a complete half-turn. This angle is formed when the rays extend in opposite directions, creating a straight line.

- **Reflex angles** measure greater than 180° but less than 360°. These angles are typically observed in complex geometric configurations and involve a more extensive rotation around the vertex.

Lines can be categorized into distinct types based on their spatial relationships and interactions:

- **Parallel lines** are characterized by maintaining a constant distance from each other, regardless of their length. These lines never intersect, and their equidistant nature is a key principle in Euclidean geometry.

- **Perpendicular lines** intersect at a right angle, forming four right angles at the point of intersection. This relationship is fundamental in constructing perpendicular bisectors and defining orthogonality in coordinate systems.

- **Intersecting lines** are lines that cross each other at any angle that is not . The point of intersection is where the lines meet, and the angles formed can vary widely, depending on the orientation of the lines.

The interaction between lines and angles is essential for solving geometric problems, particularly those involving transversals. When a transversal intersects two parallel lines, it generates several specific angle pair relationships:

- **Corresponding angles** are located on the same side of the transversal and in corresponding positions relative to the parallel lines. These angles are congruent, meaning they have equal measurements.

- **Alternate interior angles** are situated on opposite sides of the transversal and within the parallel lines. These angles are congruent and play a significant role in proving lines parallel.

- **Alternate exterior angles** are found on opposite sides of the transversal, outside the parallel lines. Like alternate interior angles, these angles are also congruent.

- **Consecutive interior angles**, also known as same-side interior angles, are on the same side of the transversal and inside the parallel lines. The sum of these angles is 180°, reflecting their supplementary nature.

Understanding these angle relationships is essential for calculating unknown angles and has practical applications in fields such as engineering and architecture. For instance, in designing and constructing electrical systems, precise angles and alignments are vital to ensure the proper functioning and safety of the system.

Perimeter & Area Formulas for 2D Shapes

Understanding the mathematical concepts of **perimeter** and **area** for two-dimensional geometrical figures is essential in various technical disciplines, such as electrical engineering, where accurate calculations are necessary for efficient layout planning and precise material estimation. This section outlines the specific formulas utilized to compute the perimeter and area of commonly encountered 2D shapes: rectangles, triangles, and circles.

Rectangle: To determine the perimeter of a rectangle, one must sum the lengths of all four sides. Given that a rectangle is characterized by two pairs of parallel sides of equal length, the formula simplifies to twice the sum of its length (l) and width (ω). This is expressed mathematically as:

$$P = 2(l + \omega)$$

For the calculation of the rectangle's area, one multiplies the length by the width, which reflects the product of the two orthogonal dimensions defining the rectangle's extent:

$$A = l \times \omega$$

Triangle: The perimeter of a triangle is calculated by adding together the lengths of its three distinct sides, denoted as a, b, and c. This is represented by the formula:

$$P = a + b + c$$

For area calculation, when the base (b) and the corresponding height (h)—the perpendicular distance from the base to the opposite vertex—are known, the area can be determined using the formula:

$$A = \frac{1}{2} bh$$

This formula derives from the fact that a triangle can be considered as half of a parallelogram when divided along one of its heights.

Circle: The perimeter of a circle, more commonly referred to as the circumference, is computed using the formula:

$$C = 2\pi r$$

where r is the radius, the distance from the center of the circle to any point on its boundary. The constant π (pi) is approximately 3.14159, representing the ratio of the circumference of any circle to its diameter. The area of a circle is calculated using the radius as well, applying the formula:

$$A = \pi r^2$$

This formula arises from the integral of infinitesimal concentric rings that compose the circle, each with a radius incrementally increasing from zero to r.

19.2 : 3D and Coordinate Geometry

Volume & Surface Area of Solids

Understanding the intricacies of calculating volume and surface area for geometric solids such as cubes and rectangular prisms is essential for professionals in the electrical domain. These calculations are fundamental for accurately estimating the quantity of materials required and efficiently managing spatial constraints during electrical installation projects. This section provides a detailed guide on computing the volume and surface area of these solids, thereby equipping you with the precise mathematical skills necessary for the International Brotherhood of Electrical Workers (IBEW) aptitude test and subsequent professional applications.

Volume quantifies the three-dimensional space enclosed within a solid object. In the case of a cube, where all edges are congruent, denoted by the variable , the formula for volume *(V)* is expressed as:

$$V = l \times l \times l = l^3$$

This cubic relationship highlights that the volume increases exponentially with the length of the cube's edge, underscoring the importance of precise measurement.

Conversely, the volume of a rectangular prism, characterized by three distinct dimensions—length (*l*), width (ω), and height (*h*)—is computed by the product of these dimensions:

$$V = l \times \omega \times h$$

This formula reflects the multiplicative nature of volume in prisms, where the space occupied is a direct function of its three orthogonal dimensions.

Surface area pertains to the aggregate area covered by all exterior faces of a solid. For a cube, each face is a square with side length , and the surface area (*A*) is calculated as:

$$A = 6 \times (l \times l) = 6l^2$$

This formula illustrates that the surface area is a linear function of the square of the side length, multiplied by six, corresponding to the number of faces.

For a rectangular prism, the surface area is derived from the sum of the areas of its six rectangular faces, calculated as:

$$A = 2(l \times \omega)2(l \times h) + 2(\omega \times h)$$

This expression accounts for each pair of opposite faces, emphasizing the necessity to consider all dimensions in determining the total surface coverage.

In practical applications, it is imperative to meticulously verify the units associated with each dimension and ensure that the calculated results are expressed in the appropriate units, such as cubic feet for volume and square feet for surface area. When addressing non-rectangular prisms, such as triangular prisms, it is crucial to first determine the precise area of the base shape using relevant geometric principles before applying the volume formula:

$$V = base\ area \times height$$

Similarly, calculating the surface area for these prisms necessitates careful attention to the geometry of the base and lateral surfaces.

Pythagorean Theorem Applications

The Pythagorean Theorem is a fundamental mathematical principle within the field of geometry, particularly significant for individuals pursuing a career in the electrical domain through the IBEW apprenticeship program. This theorem provides the mathematical framework necessary to ascertain the precise length of any side of a right triangle, contingent upon the known lengths of the other two sides. Within the context of a right-angled triangle, the theorem articulates that the square of the hypotenuse , which is the side directly opposite the right angle, is equivalent to the sum of the squares of the other two sides, denoted as a and b. This relationship is rigorously expressed through the equation $c^2 = a^2 + b^2$.

Comprehending the Pythagorean Theorem is indispensable for addressing complex, real-world scenarios encountered in electrical work, such as calculating the most efficient wiring path in a three-dimensional environment or accurately determining the diagonal distance between two points for cable installations. To proficiently apply the theorem in practical situations, adhere to the following detailed steps:

1. **Identify the Right Triangle:** Begin by verifying the presence of a right triangle within the problem context, ensuring that one of the internal angles measures precisely 90°. This verification is crucial, as the theorem is applicable exclusively to right triangles.

2. **Assign Variables to Sides:** Proceed by methodically labeling the triangle's sides, designating the two shorter sides as a and b, and the hypotenuse, the longest side, as c. It is imperative to note that the designation of a and b is interchangeable, provided that c consistently represents the side opposite the right angle, thus ensuring clarity in subsequent calculations.

3. **Apply the Theorem:** In instances where the lengths of the two shorter sides are known and the objective is to ascertain the hypotenuse, compute the sum of the squares of a and b. Subsequently, extract the square root of this sum to determine the value of c. This process is encapsulated in the formula $c = \sqrt{a^2 + b^2}$, which facilitates precise calculation of the hypotenuse.

4. **Solve for a Leg:** When the hypotenuse and one leg are known, and the task is to find the length of the remaining leg, the formula must be algebraically manipulated to iso-

late the unknown side. For instance, to calculate a, employ the rearranged equation $a = \sqrt{c^2 - b^2}$, which involves subtracting the square of the known leg from the square of the hypotenuse, followed by taking the square root of the resultant value.

5. **Practical Application:** In the context of electrical installations, the theorem is instrumental in determining the precise length of wire required to traverse a space diagonally or in ensuring that components are strategically positioned at an exact distance apart. This not only minimizes material waste but also optimizes the efficiency of the installation process, thereby highlighting the theorem's practical utility in enhancing operational accuracy and resource management.

Coordinate Geometry Basics

Aspiring electricians who are preparing for the IBEW aptitude test must possess a comprehensive understanding of coordinate geometry. This knowledge is fundamental for effectively addressing the intricate and practical challenges encountered in electrical installations and circuit design. In this section, we delve deeply into the mathematical concepts of slope, midpoint, and distance within the coordinate plane. These concepts are indispensable for managing the complexities associated with electrical work, ensuring tasks are executed with both precision and efficiency.

The slope of a line in a coordinate plane is a critical measure that quantifies the steepness or incline of the line. It specifically indicates the rate at which the line ascends or descends along the y-axis for each incremental unit of movement along the x-axis. This is calculated using the formula $m = \dfrac{y_2 - y_1}{x_2 - x_1}$, where the coordinates (x_1, y_1) and (x_2, y_2) represent two distinct points on the line. Understanding and applying this concept is crucial for electricians when determining the precise angle at which wires or conduits should be installed across varying elevations. This adherence to exact measurements ensures that installations conform to stringent safety standards and operate with optimal efficiency, thereby preventing potential hazards and maintaining system integrity.

Identifying the midpoint of a line segment that connects two points involves calculating the exact point that bisects the segment into two congruent parts. The coordinates of this midpoint M are determined using the formula $M = (\dfrac{x_1 + x_2}{2}, \dfrac{y_1 + y_2}{2})$. This calculation is particularly significant in electrical work for accurately locating the central point required for the equitable distribution of power or resources. By ensuring a balanced load distribution, electricians can minimize the risk of overload, which is essential for maintaining system reliability and preventing equipment failure.

To accurately ascertain the distance between two points on the coordinate plane, one must calculate the length of the straight line that directly connects these points. The distance d is derived using the formula $d = \sqrt{(x_2 - x_1)^2 + (y_2 - y_1)^2}$, which is based on the principles of the Pythagorean theorem. This calculation is indispensable for electricians when determining the precise length of wire required to connect two points within an electrical system. By optimizing material use through this calculation, electricians can significantly reduce waste, leading to more cost-effective and environmentally conscious practices.

Chapter 20: Applied Trigonometry

20.1: Trigonometric Basics

SOHCAHTOA Basics

SOHCAHTOA is an acronym that encapsulates the three primary trigonometric ratios: Sine, Cosine, and Tangent, which are essential tools in the field of trigonometry, particularly when working with right-angled triangles. These ratios are critical for calculating either the lengths of sides or the measures of angles within right triangles, a necessity in various applications such as electrical engineering tasks, where one might need to determine the height of a utility pole or the angle at which a ladder rests against a vertical surface.

1. **Sine (SOH):** The Sine function is defined as the ratio of the length of the side opposite the angle in question to the length of the hypotenuse of the right triangle. For a given angle θ, this relationship is mathematically represented by the equation:

$$\sin(\theta) = \frac{Length \ of \ Opposite \ Side}{Length \ of \ Hypotenuse}$$

   To apply this, one must accurately measure the length of the side directly opposite the angle and the hypotenuse, ensuring precision in measurement to maintain the integrity of subsequent calculations.

2. **Cosine (CAH):** The Cosine function relates the length of the side adjacent to the angle to the length of the hypotenuse. This ratio is expressed as:

$$\cos(\theta) = \frac{Length \ of \ Adjacent \ Side}{Length \ of \ Hypotenuse}$$

   When utilizing the Cosine ratio, it is crucial to correctly identify and measure the side that is adjacent to the angle of interest, which is not the hypotenuse, but rather the other side that forms the angle with the hypotenuse.

3. **Tangent (TOA):** The Tangent function is defined as the ratio of the length of the side opposite the angle to the length of the side adjacent to the angle. This is expressed by the equation:

$$\tan(\theta) = \frac{Length \ of \ Opposite \ Side}{Length \ of \ Adjacent \ Side}$$

   This ratio is particularly useful when the hypotenuse is not involved in the calculation, requiring only the measurements of the two legs of the triangle.

The effective application of these trigonometric ratios necessitates a systematic approach. Begin by clearly identifying the right triangle in the problem, confirming that one angle measures exactly 90°. Subsequently, ascertain which specific sides or angles are known quantities and which are the unknowns to be determined. The selection of the appropriate trigonometric ratio is contingent upon the available information; for instance, if the problem involves known lengths of the adjacent side and the angle, and the goal is to determine the length of the hypotenuse, the Cosine ratio is applicable. The formula is then rearranged to isolate and solve for the hypotenuse:

$$Hypotenuse = \frac{Length \ of \ Adjacent \ Side}{\cos(\theta)}$$

This rearrangement allows for the computation of the hypotenuse length by dividing the measured length of the adjacent side by the cosine of the given angle, ensuring that all calculations are carried out with precision to uphold the accuracy of the results.

Solving Triangles with Trigonometry

In the realm of triangle solving, trigonometry extends well beyond the foundational SOHCAHTOA principles, necessitating a meticulous and methodical approach to accurately determine unknown sides or angles within a triangle. This capability is indispensable in various practical applications, including the field of electrical engineering, where it is employed to compute the precise angle required for optimal solar panel orientation or to ascertain the height of a pole without resorting to direct measurement techniques. The success of triangle resolution is intricately linked to the adept selection of the appropriate trigonometric ratio, which is contingent upon the specific information available.

Consider a right triangle scenario in which one angle and one side length are known. The decision to utilize sine, cosine, or tangent is governed by the spatial relationship between the known side and the given angle. For instance, in a situation where the length of the side opposite the known angle is provided and the length of the hypotenuse is sought, the sine function becomes the tool of choice. The equation is then rearranged to isolate the hypotenuse, yielding:

$Hypotenuse = \frac{Opposite \ Side}{\sin(\theta)}$. This mathematical expression is instrumental in delivering precise

solutions to complex real-world problems, where exact measurements are critical.

In contrast, when the length of the adjacent side and an angle are known, and the objective is to find the length of the opposite side, the tangent function is applied. The corresponding equation, $Opposite \ Side = \tan(\theta) \times Adjacent \ Side$, provides a direct computational pathway for determining the length of the opposite side. This underscores the tangible utility of trigonometry in fieldwork scenarios, where quick and accurate calculations are often required.

When tasked with determining an unknown angle given the lengths of two sides, inverse trigonometric functions come into play. Specifically, when both the opposite and adjacent side lengths are known, the arctangent function is employed to deduce the angle: $\theta = \arctan\left(\dfrac{Opposite\ Side}{Adjacent\ Side}\right)$.

This calculation is essential for operations demanding precise angular measurements, such as in the exact alignment of a ladder against a vertical surface, thereby ensuring safety and stability.

20.2: Real-World Applications

Word Problems: Trig in Height & Distance

When confronted with word problems that involve trigonometric calculations for determining heights and distances, it is essential to deconstruct the problem into more manageable components. Begin by meticulously identifying all given variables, such as distances, angles, and any initial measurements, along with the unknown quantities that need to be determined. This step necessitates a detailed analysis of the problem statement to extract numerical values and conditions that will guide the solution process. The next critical step involves selecting the appropriate trigonometric ratio—sine, cosine, or tangent—based on the configuration of the problem and the information available. Each trigonometric function corresponds to specific sides of a right triangle relative to an angle, and the choice depends on which sides are known and which require calculation.

For instance, in scenarios where the objective is to ascertain the height of a structure using a clinometer from a predetermined horizontal distance, the tangent ratio is predominantly utilized. This is due to its direct involvement with the angle of elevation, which is measured from the horizontal ground level to the line of sight reaching the top of the building, and the horizontal distance from the observer to the base of the building. In this context, the height of the building is denoted by h, the horizontal distance from the observer to the building by d, and the angle of elevation by θ. The tangent of the angle θ is defined as the ratio of the length of the side opposite the angle, which is the height h, to the length of the adjacent side, which is the distance d. This relationship is mathematically expressed by the equation:

$$\tan(\theta) = \frac{h}{d}$$

To solve for the unknown height , the equation is algebraically manipulated to isolate on one side, resulting in:

$$h = d \cdot \tan(\theta)$$

This formulation allows for the computation of the building's height when both the distance d to the building and the angle of elevation θ are known quantities. For example, consider a scenario where the distance d is precisely measured at 100 meters, and the angle of elevation θ to the apex of the building is accurately determined to be 35°. Substituting these values into the equation provides:

$$h = 100 \cdot \tan(35°)$$

Utilizing a scientific calculator, configured to interpret angles in degrees, the tangent of 35° is calculated, yielding a result for h of approximately 70 meters. This methodology exemplifies the practical application of trigonometry in real-world scenarios, where direct measurement of heights is unfeasible. It is particularly advantageous for professionals such as electricians and other technical tradespeople who require precise height measurements for planning and executing projects. Such trigonometric techniques are integral to developing advanced problem-solving capabilities, a crucial skill set for candidates preparing for assessments like the IBEW aptitude test, which evaluates mathematical proficiency within technical contexts.

Angles of Elevation and Depression

Understanding the intricacies of angles of elevation and depression is crucial for effectively addressing real-world trigonometry problems, particularly within the electrical sector, where precise measurements are of utmost importance. These angles specifically quantify the vertical angle at which an observer must adjust their line of sight either upward or downward to view a particular object.

The angle of elevation is defined as the angle formed between a horizontal reference line and the observer's line of sight when looking upward towards an object. Consider the scenario in which one needs to determine the height of a utility pole. In this case, the angle of elevation is the angle formed between the horizontal line, which is at the observer's eye level, and the line extending from the observer's eye to the top of the pole. This geometric relationship can be expressed mathematically: if the observer is positioned at a horizontal distance d from the base of the pole, and the pole's height is denoted by h, the tangent of the angle of elevation θ is given by the equation $\tan(\theta) = \dfrac{h}{d}$. This formula arises from the definition of the tangent function in a right triangle, where the tangent of an angle is the ratio of the length of the opposite side to the length of the adjacent side.

Conversely, the angle of depression is the angle measured from a horizontal line downward to the object of interest. Imagine standing on the roof of a building and looking down at a transformer situated on the ground. Here, the angle of depression is the angle between the observer's line of sight and an imaginary horizontal line parallel to the ground. The computation of the angle of depression is analogous to that of the angle of elevation because these two angles are congruent when considered from opposite sides of the observer's line of sight, a result supported by the alternate interior angles theorem.

When solving problems that involve these angles, the initial step is to identify whether the scenario involves an angle of elevation or one of depression. Once this is established, construct a right triangle that accurately represents the situation, ensuring that the angle is positioned correctly within the triangle. Clearly label the sides of the triangle: the side opposite the angle represents the object's height, the adjacent side corresponds to the horizontal distance from the object, and the hypotenuse is the direct line of sight from the observer to the object. With this setup, apply the trigonometric ratio $\tan(\theta) = \dfrac{opposite}{adjacent}$, and use algebraic techniques to isolate and solve for the unknown value.

For instance, if it is known that the horizontal distance to a light post is 50 feet and the angle of elevation to the top of the post is 30°, one can determine the height h of the light post. This is accomplished by rearranging the tangent formula to solve for h, yielding $h = 50 \cdot \tan(30°)$. Substituting the known values into this equation allows for an accurate calculation of the height.

Calculator Shortcuts

The proficiency in utilizing calculator shortcuts is an essential skill for the effective resolution of trigonometry-related questions under the stringent time limitations of the IBEW aptitude examination. A scientific calculator equipped with the capability to process trigonometric functions is indispensable when addressing questions that involve calculating heights, distances, and angles. Presented here are detailed shortcuts and techniques designed to enhance both the speed and precision of your problem-solving abilities during the test.

Initially, it is imperative to thoroughly familiarize yourself with the specific trigonometric function keys available on your calculator: *sin*, *cos*, and *tan*, as well as their corresponding inverse functions, *sin*$^{-1}$, *cos*$^{-1}$, and *tan*$^{-1}$. Mastery of swift access to these keys can result in the conservation of critical seconds throughout the examination.

When confronted with problems that involve right triangles, the mnemonic SOHCAHTOA serves as a systematic guide for selecting the appropriate trigonometric ratio. It is advantageous to utilize the memory storage keys (M+, M-, MR, MC) for retaining intermediate computational results. For instance, in the process of determining the height h using the equation $h = d \cdot \tan(\theta)$, one should first store the distance d in the calculator's memory. Following this, directly multiply the stored value by the tangent of the angle θ, which can be efficiently retrieved from memory, thereby optimizing the calculation workflow.

Ensure that your calculator is set to the correct angular mode—either degree or radian—according to the specific requirements of the problem at hand. Given that the majority of trigonometry problems on the IBEW aptitude test are presented in degrees, it is prudent to pre-set your calculator to degree mode. This proactive adjustment negates the necessity for any subsequent conversions, thus preventing potential errors.

Leverage the calculator's built-in equation-solving capabilities for addressing equations with unknown variables. Advanced models of calculators offer the functionality to solve for an unknown directly. By inputting the complete equation and specifying the variable to solve, the calculator can deliver the solution without the need for manual algebraic manipulation, thereby significantly reducing the time spent on calculations.

Engage in regular practice sessions with your calculator to develop proficiency in swiftly entering sequences of operations. This practice not only enhances speed but also diminishes the likelihood of errors that may arise from incorrect key presses. Continuous practice with trigonometric calculations and the aforementioned shortcuts will cultivate muscle memory, ensuring that efficient calculator usage becomes instinctual during the examination.

Chapter 21: Reading Comprehension Skills

21.1: Understanding the Test & Active Reading

Reading Comprehension Basics

To excel in the Reading Comprehension section of the IBEW aptitude test, it is imperative to master the skill of dissecting nonfiction texts, which requires a systematic approach to understanding and analyzing the information presented. This proficiency is not only pivotal for passing the exam but also serves as an indispensable asset throughout the apprenticeship and into one's professional journey in the electrical field. Nonfiction texts, particularly those related to technical subjects, are meticulously structured to convey information, instructions, or data in a manner that is both clear and logical. Extracting meaning from these texts necessitates the application of several key strategies: identifying the main idea, understanding the structure, and discerning the author's purpose.

The main idea of a passage represents the central concept or argument that the author intends to communicate to the reader. This main idea is frequently explicitly stated within the introduction or conclusion of the text; however, in some instances, it may be implied through the use of supporting details and illustrative examples. To accurately pinpoint the main idea, one must consider the overarching message the author aims for the reader to grasp. This practice is particularly beneficial in technical texts where the main idea often revolves around the solution to a specific problem or an explanation of a complex process.

To thoroughly comprehend the structure of nonfiction texts, it is essential to recognize the specific organizational pattern the author employs to present the information. Common organizational structures include chronological, where events or steps are presented in the order they occur; cause and effect, which explores the relationship between events or actions and their outcomes; compare and contrast, which highlights similarities and differences between two or more subjects; and problem and solution, which outlines a problem followed by one or more solutions. Recognizing these patterns aids in anticipating the type of details that may follow, allowing for a more efficient mental organization of the information, which is crucial for accurately and efficiently answering test questions.

Determining the author's purpose is another critical aspect of reading comprehension. An author might aim to inform by providing factual information, to explain by detailing how something works, or to persuade by convincing the reader of a particular viewpoint. Identifying the purpose of the text assists in understanding the tone and the choice of details included by the author. For instance, instructional texts, which are prevalent in technical fields, aim to elucidate processes or methods in a step-by-step manner, with a focus on clarity and precision to ensure the reader can replicate the described procedures accurately.

Active reading techniques, such as annotating the text, summarizing paragraphs, and asking questions, significantly enhance comprehension and retention of the material. These strategies foster engagement with the content, making it easier to identify relevant details and main ideas. Practicing with a diverse array of texts, including workplace documents, technical manuals, and informational articles, prepares test-takers for the variety of reading materials they will encounter on the exam and in their future careers.

Types of Texts on the Test

The IBEW aptitude test is designed with a variety of text types specifically structured to evaluate your proficiency in reading comprehension, a skill essential for thriving in the electrical industry. A comprehensive understanding of these texts, coupled with consistent practice, can significantly enhance your performance on the test.

Texts related to workplace scenarios are crafted to replicate the kind of reading material you will frequently encounter in your role as an electrician, including, but not limited to, safety manuals, detailed technical specifications, and exhaustive project documentation. To master these texts, it is imperative to focus on identifying precise details that are vital for executing tasks both safely and accurately. For instance, a safety manual may meticulously delineate the protocol for de-energizing electrical circuits prior to conducting maintenance work, highlighting the exact sequence of steps to be followed and the critical safety precautions to be observed. This may involve understanding the specific order in which circuit breakers must be switched off, the application of lockout/tagout procedures to ensure circuits remain de-energized, and the verification of zero voltage using appropriate testing equipment.

Instructional texts are designed to provide guidance on executing tasks or operations, organized in a manner that conveys information logically and sequentially. It is essential to pay close attention to the order of actions required and any conditional statements that may be present, such as "if-then" scenarios that are prevalent in troubleshooting guides. Understanding the progression of these instructions equips you to tackle questions that inquire about predicting possible outcomes or determining the correct sequence of actions. For example, a troubleshooting guide might instruct that if a circuit does not energize, then one should first check the continuity of the wiring, followed by inspecting the circuit breaker status, and ultimately verifying the integrity of the power supply.

Informational texts are intended to elucidate concepts, processes, or theories pertinent to the electrical trade, encompassing subjects such as the fundamental principles of electricity, the historical evolution of electrical engineering, or recent advancements in electrical technology. The challenge lies in extracting the core idea, comprehending the supporting details, and discerning the author's intent. It is crucial to distinguish between factual information, subjective opinions, and theoretical hypotheses, especially when engaging with discussions on emerging technologies or speculative concepts. This may involve recognizing the difference between a factual statement about the conductivity of certain materials and an opinion on the future potential of superconductors in power transmission.

To achieve excellence in the reading comprehension section, it is beneficial to engage with a diverse array of texts. Practice active reading techniques by annotating key points, summarizing paragraphs succinctly, and posing questions regarding the author's intent and the underlying meaning of the text. This active engagement will aid in navigating complex texts more effectively, thereby enhancing your comprehension and retention of the material.

Active Reading Techniques

Active reading techniques are integral to enhancing both comprehension and retention, particularly when preparing for the IBEW aptitude test. This section delves into specific strategies designed to maintain engagement with the text, enabling the identification of critical concepts and the formulation of insightful questions that facilitate a more profound grasp of the material.

Engage dynamically with the text by employing a methodical approach to questioning it. Prior to delving into the material, conduct a preliminary scan to formulate targeted questions such as, "What specific problem is the author attempting to address?" or "Which particular methods are being proposed for this issue?" This approach establishes a clear objective for your reading session, channeling your attention towards uncovering precise answers. As you navigate through the text, continue to interrogate the author's arguments by examining the validity of their evidence and the soundness of their conclusions. This active inquiry not only fosters critical thinking but also aids in distinguishing between central ideas and ancillary supporting details, thereby ensuring a comprehensive understanding of the material.

Highlight and annotate the text meticulously to denote pivotal points and personal insights. Develop a detailed system of symbols or colors to distinctly categorize crucial concepts, terminologies, or sections that warrant further scrutiny. This technique not only facilitates rapid reference but also visually delineates the text's structure, thus simplifying the process of following the progression of ideas. For instance, use a specific color for definitions, another for examples, and different symbols to indicate connections or contradictions within the text.

Summarize paragraphs or sections in your own words to ensure a deep comprehension of the content. This practice requires you to distill information into its core components, thereby verifying your understanding of the material. Write these summaries either in the margins or in a dedicated notebook, providing a concise yet comprehensive review resource that captures the essence of the text without extraneous detail.

Enhance understanding and memory retention by constructing mind maps or concept maps derived from the text. Create detailed diagrams that link the central idea with associated concepts and supporting details. These visual representations serve to distill complex information into a more manageable format, facilitating easier recall and deeper understanding. Ensure that each node in your map is clearly labeled and that connections are logically structured to accurately reflect the relationships between concepts.

Predict outcomes and draw reasoned conclusions based on the text before they are explicitly articulated to exercise your deductive reasoning skills. This anticipatory reading strategy is designed to prepare you for the critical thinking questions encountered on the IBEW aptitude test, thereby deepening your comprehension of the material. By actively forecasting potential conclusions, you engage more thoroughly with the text, honing your ability to synthesize information and apply logical reasoning to anticipate the author's trajectory.

21.2: Identifying Main Ideas and Purpose

Finding the Main Idea

To effectively pinpoint the primary concept within a passage, it is essential to distill the text to its fundamental message, a process that involves isolating and synthesizing the most critical information presented. This capability is particularly vital for the International Brotherhood of Electrical Workers (IBEW) aptitude test, where the ability to comprehend and accurately interpret technical material can significantly influence the outcome. Typically, the main idea is encapsulated in a thesis statement, which is often strategically positioned within the introduction or conclusion of the passage. However, it may also require inference derived from a synthesis of pivotal points distributed throughout the text.

Commence by meticulously reading the passage, directing focused attention towards the initial and concluding sentences of each paragraph. These sentences frequently encapsulate the essence of the author's intended message. In instances where the main idea is not overtly articulated, compile a list of significant points expressed in each section. Identify the recurring theme or concept that cohesively binds these points, as it is likely to represent the main idea.

When confronted with intricate passages, especially those containing technical descriptions or procedural instructions, segment the text into smaller, more manageable portions. After thoroughly reading each segment, pose the question, "What is the author attempting to communicate in this section?" Condense your response into a concise sentence. This exercise compels you to actively engage with the information, facilitating a deeper understanding by articulating it in your own words, thereby enhancing comprehension.

Engage with the text in a proactive manner. Annotate or make notes in the margins to emphasize critical terms, precise definitions, and statements that highlight the passage's central point. This approach fosters sustained focus and facilitates the connection of disparate sections within the text, thereby enhancing overall understanding.

Assess the author's intent. Determine whether the text's primary objective is to inform, persuade, or elucidate a process. Comprehending the author's purpose can yield valuable insights into the main idea, as the content is typically organized to fulfill this objective. In texts that are instructional in nature, the main idea frequently centers around the methodology for executing a specific task or resolving a problem, supported by detailed steps or methods outlined within the text.

Consistent practice is indispensable. Applying these strategies across a diverse array of texts will refine your proficiency in swiftly and accurately identifying the main idea, thereby aiding in test preparation and enhancing competencies in the electrical trade. This is particularly crucial, as interpreting technical documents accurately is imperative for ensuring both safety and operational efficiency.

Author's Purpose and Tone

Understanding the underlying intention of an author and discerning the specific tone employed in a text are critical competencies for engaging effectively with reading materials, particularly when preparing for the International Brotherhood of Electrical Workers (IBEW) aptitude test. Authors craft their works with distinct objectives: to inform, to explain, or to instruct, each serving a unique function in the realm of communication. Identifying these objectives enables readers to adjust their anticipations accordingly, facilitating a more targeted extraction of pertinent information.

When an author seeks to inform, they aim to furnish the reader with factual content, empirical data, or objective information, devoid of any intention to alter the reader's beliefs or actions. Texts with an informative purpose are generally direct and unambiguous, meticulously presenting factual, objective details. For instance, a technical document detailing the electrical conductivity properties of various materials is designed to expand the reader's knowledge base, providing precise measurements, comparisons, and scientific explanations, without attempting to sway the reader towards any particular viewpoint or decision.

In scenarios where the author's goal is to explain, the text is structured to elucidate a concept or process, frequently deconstructing complex subjects into more digestible components. This approach is prevalent in materials that delve into theories or intricate concepts, where comprehension hinges on the reader's ability to follow a logical sequence of ideas. The tone in such texts is typically more engaging and interactive, often employing illustrative examples, detailed analogies, or step-by-step breakdowns to bridge potential gaps in understanding and facilitate a deeper grasp of the subject matter.

Instructional texts, crafted with the intention of teaching the reader how to execute a specific task, are ubiquitous in technical disciplines such as electrical work. These materials are distinguished by a directive tone, frequently utilizing an imperative voice that provides unambiguous, sequential instructions. Recognizing this instructional purpose equips readers to engage with the text from a practical standpoint, ready to implement the instructions in real-world applications. The clarity and precision of the language used in such texts are paramount, ensuring that each step is comprehensible and actionable, thereby minimizing the risk of errors in execution.

The tone of a text can exhibit considerable variation, ranging from formal and objective in informational texts to conversational and subjective in opinion pieces. Tone significantly influences how the information is perceived and interpreted by the reader. A formal tone, commonly found in technical descriptions or official guidelines, conveys a sense of authority and engenders confidence in the credibility of the information presented. In contrast, a more casual tone might be employed in materials designed to make complex subjects more approachable for beginners, aiming to diminish intimidation and create an inviting learning environment. This casual tone may incorporate relatable language, simplified explanations, and a supportive narrative to encourage engagement and comprehension.

To accurately identify the author's purpose and tone, it is essential to engage actively with the text. This involves scrutinizing the language employed, analyzing the structure of the information presented, and considering the context in which the material is delivered. For instance, an instructional manual on safety protocols will likely adopt a direct, imperative tone, underscoring the importance of each procedural step to ensure adherence to safe practices. Recognizing these elements enhances the reader's ability to comprehend the material at hand and equips them with the skills necessary to navigate a diverse array of texts, from technical manuals to theoretical discussions, with increased proficiency and insight.

Topic Sentences and Traps

Mastering reading comprehension for the IBEW aptitude test necessitates a meticulous approach to identifying **topic sentences**, which are critical for understanding the core message within a paragraph. These sentences, often strategically placed, encapsulate the primary concept or argument the author wishes to convey, serving as a navigational tool through the text's logical structure. Recognizing these sentences requires attention to their typical positioning and function. Although they are frequently located at the beginning of a paragraph, indicating the forthcoming discussion, topic sentences can also appear at the end, summarizing the preceding information, or occasionally in the middle, signaling a pivotal transition in the narrative. The key to pinpointing these sentences lies in identifying those that articulate a comprehensive idea or a general opinion, around which the paragraph's subsequent details are organized. For instance, a sentence such as, "The advent of renewable energy sources has significantly impacted electrical engineering practices," suggests a paragraph that will elaborate on various ways renewable energy has influenced these practices, thus guiding the reader to anticipate a detailed exploration of this impact.

Conversely, identifying and avoiding **traps** is crucial, as these can lead to misinterpretations or incorrect responses. Traps often manifest as sentences that are overly specific or tangential, masquerading as the main idea by focusing on minute details or introducing tangential information that, while related, strays from the central theme of the paragraph. For example, a sentence that delves into the specific outcomes of a single renewable energy project, if positioned as a focal point, might mislead the reader into perceiving it as the paragraph's main idea, rather than understanding it as a supporting example that illustrates a broader concept.

To effectively navigate these traps and enhance comprehension, several strategies can be employed:

- **Read in Context:** Engage with the potential topic sentence by examining it within the broader context of the entire paragraph. Assess whether it encapsulates the paragraph's overall content or merely represents one of several specific examples. This involves a careful analysis of how the sentence interacts with surrounding details to form a cohesive argument or narrative.

- **Verify with Details:** Once a potential topic sentence has been identified, scrutinize each subsequent detail in the paragraph to ensure they collectively support or expand upon the identified sentence. If the details appear disjointed or unrelated, it may indicate the presence of a trap, prompting a reevaluation of the initial choice.

- **Clarify the Author's Intent:** Delve into the underlying intent of the author by questioning what message or argument they aim to communicate within the paragraph. If the initial topic sentence does not align with this intent, consider whether another sentence more accurately reflects the paragraph's purpose. This involves a critical examination of the text to discern the author's overarching objective and ensure alignment with the identified topic sentence.

21.3: Details, Evidence, and Organization

Supporting Details

Grasping and pinpointing supporting details in a text is a critical skill for thoroughly understanding the main idea and reinforcing the author's intended message. These details serve as foundational elements of the main idea, providing necessary evidence, illustrative examples, and comprehensive explanations that make the central concept more tangible and convincingly argued. When preparing for the IBEW aptitude test, the ability to discern these elements is instrumental in accurately comprehending reading passages and effectively answering questions.

Supporting details manifest in multiple forms, including but not limited to statistical data, anecdotal evidence, factual statements, and logical reasoning. For instance, if a passage asserts that modern safety standards have significantly decreased electrical hazards in the workplace, supporting details might encompass quantitative data illustrating a decline in workplace accidents over a specified time frame, examples of newly implemented safety protocols adopted across various industries, or detailed explanations of the mechanisms by which these protocols mitigate accident risks. Such details may include specific statistics, such as a percentage reduction in electrical-related injuries following the introduction of new safety measures, or a case study of a particular company that successfully reduced its incident rate by adopting these standards.

To effectively identify these details, readers should initially ascertain the main idea of the passage or paragraph by pinpointing the overarching statement or concept the author seeks to communicate. Once the main idea is discerned, the reader can meticulously scan the text for sentences or phrases that bolster it. It is imperative to distinguish between pertinent supporting details and superfluous information that does not contribute to the core argument. This involves analyzing each piece of information to determine its relevance to the main idea and its role in substantiating the author's claims.

Readers can employ a systematic approach by posing questions such as "Why?" or "How?" in relation to the main idea. If the main idea presents a fact or opinion, the supporting details should elucidate the reasoning behind it or substantiate its validity. For example, if the main idea posits that advancements in technology have enhanced the efficiency of electrical systems, supporting details might delineate how specific technological innovations, such as the integration of smart grid technology or the adoption of energy-efficient components, have led to these improvements. This could involve providing examples of electrical systems that have experienced measurable efficiency gains due to such advancements, along with technical descriptions of the innovations themselves.

Another crucial aspect is the organization of these details within the text. Authors frequently arrange supporting details in a logical sequence, such as prioritizing information from most to least important, presenting it chronologically, or categorizing it into distinct groups or lists. Recognizing this structural organization can significantly aid readers in processing and retaining the information presented. For instance, a chronological arrangement might trace the evolution of safety standards over time, while a categorical approach might group details by type of innovation or industry application, thereby facilitating a more nuanced understanding of the subject matter.

Logical Flow of Ideas

Grasping the logical flow of ideas within a text is essential for dissecting its intricate structure and extracting its nuanced meaning, particularly when preparing for the International Brotherhood of Electrical Workers (IBEW) aptitude test. This comprehension involves a meticulous analysis of how each discrete idea interconnects to construct a cohesive narrative or argument. The logical flow serves as the skeletal framework of a text, underpinning all details, evidence, and organizational elements. Recognizing this flow enables readers to anticipate the trajectory of the text, thus enhancing both comprehension and retention of the material.

To dissect the logical flow, one should begin by identifying the thesis or principal argument, typically articulated at the outset. This statement functions as the foundational anchor for all subsequent information. The author systematically presents various supporting points or evidence, meticulously structured to reinforce the initial premise. The structure may adhere to a cause-and-effect pattern, a problem-solution framework, or a chronological sequence, depending on the text's specific purpose and objectives.

Consider a passage detailing the evolution of electrical safety standards. The logical flow might commence with an exposition of the historical context surrounding electrical safety, followed by a comprehensive account of significant advancements in safety technology. The text could then delineate current challenges and potential future developments, each section transitioning logically from past events toward future prospects, thereby maintaining a clear and systematic sequence that facilitates comprehension.

Transitional phrases such as "furthermore," "however," or "consequently" are indispensable for signaling shifts in the narrative or argument, effectively guiding the reader through the logical progression of ideas. These linguistic cues function as bridges between different sections of the text, ensuring a seamless transition between topics and maintaining the reader's engagement with the material.

Examining paragraph structure is also critical. A well-organized paragraph initiates with a topic sentence that introduces the main idea, followed by sentences that furnish detailed supporting information, and concludes with a sentence that either encapsulates the main point or transitions to the subsequent idea. This micro-level structure mirrors the macro-level flow of the entire text, with each paragraph acting as a fundamental building block in the overarching argument or narrative.

To augment understanding of a text's logical flow, readers can actively summarize each paragraph's primary point before proceeding to the next. This exercise reinforces the connection between individual ideas and the text's overarching thesis. Interrogating the purpose of each paragraph and its contribution to the text's overall argument can further elucidate the logical flow, rendering even the most complex texts more accessible and comprehensible.

Eliminating Wrong Answers

Eliminating incorrect answers is a crucial competency for effectively navigating the IBEW aptitude test, particularly within the reading comprehension segment. This skill relies on the ability to discern between answer choices that accurately encapsulate the author's intended message and those that distort it. To proficiently eliminate incorrect options, one must engage in rigorous analytical thinking and possess a comprehensive understanding of the passage's content.

Commence by scrutinizing the presence of absolute terms within the answer choices. Terms such as "always," "never," "all," and "none" signify absolute assertions. In technical texts, the complexity of real-world scenarios seldom aligns with absolute statements. If an answer choice employs an absolute term while the passage conveys information with subtlety and nuance, this serves as a strong indicator of its incorrectness.

Proceed to evaluate the scope and pertinence of each answer. An incorrect choice may present information that, although generally accurate, lacks direct relevance to the specific details articulated in the passage. For instance, if the passage focuses on the efficiency parameters of a particular electrical system, an answer that broadly addresses electrical systems without direct correlation to the passage's specific context may act as a diversion.

Exercise caution with distortions or exaggerations of the passage's assertions. Certain options may offer a conclusion or fact that appears credible but is, in reality, an exaggerated form of what the text conveys. Conduct a meticulous comparison of each choice with the text to ensure that the answer neither amplifies nor diminishes the author's original points.

Misplaced details frequently yield incorrect answers. These details might be factually accurate and present within the passage but fail to address the question's core intent. It is imperative to align the answer not only with the passage's content but also with the precise focus of the question being asked.

Engage in critical reading by rigorously questioning the validity of each answer choice. Deliberate on whether the answer choice is directly supported by the text and whether it most accurately represents the author's principal argument or point. This method fosters a deeper engagement with the material, thereby enhancing one's ability to identify and eliminate incorrect answers with precision.

21.4 : Making Inferences

Inference Skills

The development of robust inference skills is an essential component for effectively interpreting reading passages, particularly in the context of the IBEW aptitude test. Inference, in this setting, refers to the intellectual process of drawing conclusions that are supported by evidence and logical reasoning, rather than relying solely on information that is explicitly stated within the text. This cognitive skill is pivotal as it allows for the comprehension of nuanced meanings and implicit messages embedded within the text, thereby enhancing one's analytical capabilities and depth of understanding.

To achieve proficiency in making inferences, it is imperative to engage with the text in a deliberate and methodical manner. This involves a meticulous examination of textual clues that may suggest broader themes, underlying attitudes, or contextual frameworks. Such clues can manifest through the use of descriptive language, the tone employed by the author, or the intricate relationships between presented ideas and factual content. For instance, in a passage detailing a worker's meticulous adherence to safety protocols, one might infer the critical importance of safety within the realm of electrical work, despite the absence of an explicit statement to that effect.

Grasping the contextual framework of the text is another critical element of inference. Background information, whether historical, cultural, or technical, can provide substantial insights into the author's perspective or the specific situation being depicted. For example, an understanding of historical developments in electrical standards might illuminate the progression of safety measures over time, thereby enriching the reader's comprehension of the text's implications.

Engaging in a comparative analysis of statements within the text is also beneficial for making inferences. Authors may strategically juxtapose two ideas to underscore a particular point or to highlight a significant change or development. By scrutinizing these comparisons, one can infer the broader significance of these ideas within the overall context of the passage, thereby gaining a deeper understanding of the author's intent.

A critical approach involves questioning why the author has chosen to incorporate certain details or depict events in a particular manner. This inquisitive method fosters a more profound engagement with the text and can uncover hidden themes or messages that might otherwise go unnoticed.

Consistent practice is crucial for honing inference skills. Exposure to a diverse array of reading materials, including technical manuals, informational texts, and narrative passages, is recommended. Following each reading, challenge yourself to distill not only the information that is overtly presented but also the subtleties and implications that are woven into the text. This rigorous practice will enhance your capacity to formulate logical conclusions based on the available information and your own analytical reasoning.

Types of Inference Questions

In the specific context of the IBEW aptitude test, particularly within its reading comprehension section, candidates are presented with a diverse array of inference questions meticulously crafted to evaluate their proficiency in deducing logical conclusions from the provided text. These questions are systematically categorized into three distinct types: assumption, implication, and prediction. It is essential for candidates to thoroughly understand the subtle distinctions of each question type to effectively navigate this section.

Assumption questions necessitate that the reader discerns unstated premises upon which the author's argument is constructed. For example, if a passage elaborates on the advantages of employing a particular type of safety equipment in electrical work, an assumption question might require the candidate to identify the underlying beliefs the author holds regarding the importance of workplace safety standards. To tackle such questions, candidates should carefully search for textual cues that indicate a broader principle or belief subtly influencing the author's viewpoint. This involves a thorough analysis of the language and context to reveal foundational ideas that are crucial for maintaining the argument's internal coherence and logical integrity.

Implication questions require the reader to determine what the text indirectly suggests or implies without direct articulation. These questions frequently demand an interpretation of the wider significance of specific details or an understanding of the potential ramifications of the presented information. For instance, if a passage describes the implementation of a novel electrical code, an implication question might explore the potential effects this code could have on existing training practices within the industry. Success in answering these questions hinges on the ability to extrapolate from the explicit information provided, thereby enabling the candidate to anticipate broader impacts or derive nuanced meanings that are not immediately apparent.

Prediction questions engage the reader in forecasting future developments grounded in the passage's content. This might involve predicting the outcome of a trend explicitly described in the text or anticipating subsequent steps in a process or argument. For instance, a passage might delineate the current challenges confronting the electrical industry, and a prediction question could prompt the reader to propose likely future advancements in safety technology. Addressing these questions demands a comprehensive synthesis of the passage's details, requiring the candidate to construct a logical progression into future scenarios based on the information at hand.

Avoid Overthinking

In the context of reading comprehension, particularly relevant to the IBEW aptitude test, it is imperative to avoid the cognitive trap of overanalyzing or overthinking the material presented. This entails drawing conclusions that are strictly anchored in the textual evidence provided, without allowing assumptions or external knowledge to interfere and potentially skew the interpretation of the content.

To adhere to this principle, one must concentrate meticulously on the explicit information contained within the text. For instance, consider a passage that elaborates on the efficiency of a newly introduced electrical tool. It is essential to scrutinize the text for specific features or outcomes that are described, such as the tool's energy consumption levels, durability in various conditions, or its impact on workflow efficiency. One should refrain from allowing personal opinions or prior experiences with analogous tools to influence interpretation, thereby ensuring that any conclusions drawn are firmly rooted in the passage's explicit content.

When making inferences, it is crucial to confine them to what the text reasonably suggests. Suppose the passage hints at a particular advantage of using a specific electrical component, such as enhanced safety measures. In such cases, limit your inference to this explicitly mentioned benefit. Refrain from extrapolating to other advantages, such as potential cost savings or the simplicity of installation, unless these aspects are also directly implied or discussed within the text.

Utilizing a comparative analysis of statements within the passage can be an effective strategy to mitigate overthinking. This method involves a detailed examination of how various pieces of information interrelate to accurately decode the author's intended message. For example, if the text draws a comparison between traditional and modern wiring techniques, focus on dissecting the specific points of comparison, such as differences in material conductivity, installation time, or safety standards, rather than introducing extraneous knowledge about the broader evolution of electrical standards.

Engaging in practice exercises can significantly refine one's ability to avoid overthinking. Tackle passages that necessitate making inferences, and subsequently undertake a thorough review of your cognitive process. Did you inadvertently introduce assumptions that were unsupported by the text? Were your conclusions intricately linked to the passage's explicit content? This reflective practice, focusing on identifying and correcting these tendencies, will progressively enhance your capacity to remain within the confines of the information provided, thereby improving both accuracy and comprehension.

21.5: Contextual Vocabulary

Using Context Clues

Mastering the skill of using context clues is essential for accurately deciphering unfamiliar words encountered in technical and workplace texts, particularly when preparing for the International Brotherhood of Electrical Workers (IBEW) aptitude test. Context clues are strategically embedded hints within the surrounding text that facilitate the inference of an unknown word's meaning without the necessity of consulting a dictionary. This technique not only conserves valuable time but also significantly enhances comprehension and retention of the material being studied, which is critical in high-pressure testing environments.

There are several distinct types of context clues that can be identified: definitions, synonyms, antonyms, examples, and the general sense of the passage. Definitions are often presented immediately following an unfamiliar term, typically introduced by phrases such as "which means" or "referred to as." For example, in a technical passage, if the term "conduit" is introduced and followed by the phrase "a protective tube through which wires are run," the segment following "conduit" provides a direct and explicit definition, clarifying the function and purpose of the term within the context of electrical work.

Synonyms are utilized when a sentence presents an unfamiliar word and subsequently restates it using a more familiar term, frequently connected by conjunctions such as "or" or separated by a comma. For instance, consider the sentence: "The electrician used a multimeter, or a device that measures electrical current, to test the circuit." In this context, "device that measures electrical current" serves as a synonymous expression that elucidates the function of a multimeter, thereby providing clarity on its application in electrical diagnostics.

Antonyms are employed when the text introduces a word opposite in meaning to the unfamiliar term, typically signaled by contrastive words such as "however," "but," or "unlike." This method aids in inferring the meaning by delineating what the term does not represent. For example, if a passage states, "The wire was flexible, unlike the rigid conduit," the term "rigid" serves as an antonym to "flexible," offering insight into the properties of the conduit.

Examples serve to clarify the unknown word by enumerating specific instances, often introduced by phrases such as "such as," "for example," or "including." These examples provide tangible illustrations that concretize abstract concepts, enhancing understanding by linking the unfamiliar term to recognizable situations or items. For instance, in a technical context, a sentence might read, "Insulating materials, such as rubber and plastic, are used to prevent electrical shock," where "rubber and plastic" are examples that elucidate the broader category of insulating materials.

The general sense or inference derived from the passage involves synthesizing information from the entire paragraph or section to hypothesize the meaning of the word. This requires a comprehensive approach, considering how the word integrates into the broader topic being discussed, and involves analyzing the context, tone, and purpose of the passage to construct an informed guess regarding the word's meaning. This method is particularly useful in complex technical documents where precise definitions may not be explicitly provided.

To employ context clues effectively, it is imperative to engage actively with the text by posing questions such as "What hints are provided about this word?" or "How does this word relate to the overall topic?" This active engagement involves scrutinizing the text for linguistic markers and structural cues that offer insights into the unfamiliar word. Practicing this skill involves systematically identifying unfamiliar words in technical manuals or informational texts and meticulously using the surrounding information to infer their meanings, thereby enhancing one's ability to navigate complex technical language with proficiency.

Eliminating Incorrect Word Choices

Eliminating incorrect word choices is an essential skill for enhancing reading comprehension, especially when preparing for the IBEW aptitude test, which evaluates one's ability to discern and apply technical language accurately. This skill relies on the precise application of logical reasoning and a comprehensive understanding of grammatical rules to meticulously evaluate each potential meaning and identify the definition that aligns most accurately with the context presented in the passage. The procedure involves a systematic examination of each word choice, rigorously assessing its relevance and precision within the specific structural and thematic framework of the text.

To effectively eliminate incorrect word choices, initiate the process by discerning the part of speech necessitated by the sentence's syntactic structure. For example, if the sentence construction requires a noun, focus solely on word choices that fulfill this grammatical role, thereby excluding verbs, adjectives, or adverbs from consideration. Consider the sentence, "The electrician used a _____ to ensure the circuit was grounded." In this context, the blank necessitates a noun, facilitating the immediate exclusion of any verb, adjective, or adverb options, thus streamlining the decision-making process.

Subsequently, employ contextual logic by evaluating the technical and thematic elements inherent to the passage. If the passage pertains to electrical safety measures, the selected word choice should align with this overarching theme. Words that are extraneous to the domain of electrical work or safety protocols can be systematically eliminated due to their thematic incongruity. This step necessitates a foundational understanding of the subject matter and the capacity to extrapolate the broader context from the surrounding text, utilizing domain-specific knowledge to inform the elimination process.

Scrutinize linguistic cues, such as prepositions, articles, and conjunctions, which may provide subtle indications regarding the appropriate word choice. For instance, the presence of the article "an" preceding the blank suggests that the subsequent word should commence with a vowel sound, thereby further refining the range of potential options.

A thorough comprehension of the intricacies of technical vocabulary is imperative. Numerous technical terms possess meanings that diverge from their colloquial usage, necessitating familiarity with the specialized lexicon associated with electrical work. This familiarity enables the identification of contextually appropriate words and those that are not, based on their technical application.

Engagement with real-world examples serves as an invaluable tool for honing this skill. Regular practice with technical manuals, instructional texts, and practice tests can enhance your proficiency in swiftly and accurately eliminating incorrect word choices. Such practice not only expands your technical vocabulary but also deepens your grammatical understanding and sharpens your logical reasoning abilities, all of which are indispensable for excelling on the IBEW aptitude test.

Technical Vocabulary in Context

Grasping technical vocabulary within context requires an intricate understanding of not only the specific terms but also the broader concepts they represent, particularly in the field of electrical work. This ability is essential for aspiring electricians who are preparing for the International Brotherhood of Electrical Workers (IBEW) aptitude test, as it enables them to navigate complex informational texts and technical manuals with enhanced accuracy and efficiency. The process of deciphering job-related terminology from context is integral to test preparation and constitutes a critical component of the foundational skill set necessary for addressing future professional challenges in the industry.

In-depth analysis of technical vocabulary necessitates a thorough examination of each term within its operational context. For example, the term "ampacity" specifically denotes the maximum current, measured in amperes, that a conductor is capable of carrying continuously without exceeding its temperature rating under specific conditions of use. The context surrounding ampacity may include detailed information about a particular wiring scenario, such as ambient temperature, the type of insulation used, conductor material, and installation environment. These factors are essential for understanding the practical implications of ampacity in electrical installations, as they directly affect the safe and efficient operation of electrical systems.

Consider the term "ground fault circuit interrupter (GFCI)." The context in which this term is used can significantly affect its interpretation. When referenced in relation to electrical outlets located in bathrooms or outdoor settings, the focus is typically on safety measures designed to prevent electric shock. This is accomplished by swiftly interrupting the power supply in the event of a ground fault. A comprehensive understanding of the operational principle of a GFCI is vital, which involves monitoring the current flow on the hot side and comparing it to the current on the neutral side. If a discrepancy is detected, indicating a potential ground fault, the GFCI will disconnect the power, underscoring its critical role in electrical safety protocols.

To effectively practice interpreting technical vocabulary in context, it is beneficial to engage with a diverse array of texts that incorporate these terms in practical scenarios. Technical manuals, safety guidelines, and detailed technical descriptions provide rich opportunities to observe the application of these terms. Close attention should be paid to surrounding cues, such as detailed descriptions of processes, specific safety precautions, and precise equipment specifications, which can offer valuable insights into the practical significance and application of the term.

Adopting a systematic approach to dissecting sentences or paragraphs containing unfamiliar technical terms can significantly enhance comprehension. This involves identifying the main subject of the sentence, pinpointing verbs that indicate actions or relationships, and analyzing surrounding phrases that describe conditions, consequences, or additional details. This methodical breakdown aids in constructing a comprehensive understanding of the term's meaning and practical application within the specific context.

21.6 : Technical and Workplace Texts

Reading Instructions and Manuals

Mastering the intricate steps, detailed structure, and precise sequence inherent in technical writing is paramount for aspiring electricians preparing for the IBEW aptitude test. These documents serve as the foundational framework for electrical work, offering comprehensive guidance on the intricacies of installation procedures, troubleshooting techniques, and stringent safety protocols. The ability to accurately interpret and apply this information is not merely beneficial for success in the test; it is also critical for effective performance in real-world electrical tasks.

Technical manuals and instructions are meticulously crafted to present complex information in a logical and sequential manner. Typically, these documents commence with an introductory section that succinctly outlines the specific purpose and precise scope of the tasks to be covered. This is often followed by a detailed list of required tools and materials, functioning as a preparatory checklist. This checklist is not merely a formality; it is a critical component that ensures the electrician is fully equipped with the necessary items, thereby minimizing the risk of interruptions or delays during task execution.

The core content of these documents usually comprises procedural steps, each presented with meticulous detail to guide the user through the task at hand. These steps are frequently organized in a numbered or bulleted format to underscore the importance of the sequence in which actions must be performed. Adhering strictly to these steps in the prescribed order is crucial, as each action is often contingent upon the successful completion of the preceding one, thereby ensuring the successful completion of the task. For instance, in the context of wiring a residential circuit, the manual might explicitly detail the sequence for connecting wires to the circuit breaker, followed by the grounding process, and culminating in the testing of the connection to ensure safety. Deviating from the prescribed order or omitting steps can lead to significant errors or create safety hazards.

Diagrams and illustrations are frequently integrated into the textual instructions, providing essential visual representations of the task. These visuals are indispensable for comprehending complex procedures, as they offer graphical depictions of components, detailed wiring routes, and the final assembly configurations. The ability to interpret these diagrams involves recognizing standardized symbols, understanding the scale and proportions, and correlating these visual elements with the corresponding textual instructions. This skill is vital for enhancing both comprehension and execution accuracy.

Safety warnings and precautions are integral components of technical documents, specifically highlighting potential risks and the necessary measures to mitigate them. These sections must not be overlooked, as disregarding these warnings can result in personal injury or cause damage to equipment. Consequently, it is imperative for aspiring electricians to thoroughly read and internalize safety instructions to ensure both personal safety and the integrity of the electrical systems on which they work.

Cause and Effect in Procedures

Understanding the intricate interplay of cause and effect within technical procedures is of paramount importance for electricians, particularly when preparing for the IBEW aptitude test. This fundamental concept serves as a critical foundation in the process of troubleshooting and effectively navigating technical manuals. Each step within these manuals can trigger a distinct outcome, making it essential to comprehend this dynamic thoroughly. For instance, consider an electrical manual that provides detailed instructions on the installation of a circuit breaker. The manual might specify, "If the circuit breaker is not properly seated in the panel, it may fail to provide adequate protection against circuit overload." In this scenario, the improper seating of the circuit breaker has a direct and immediate consequence: the failure to protect against circuit overload. This failure occurs because the circuit breaker, when not seated correctly, cannot effectively interrupt the flow of electricity during an overload condition, thereby compromising the protective mechanism designed to prevent overheating and potential damage to the electrical system.

By identifying and understanding these cause-and-effect relationships, individuals can predict the outcomes of specific actions and fully appreciate the critical importance of each procedural step. Consider another example where a manual describes the process of grounding an electrical system. The instructions might read, "Connect the grounding wire to the grounding rod to prevent electrical shock in case of a fault." In this case, the action of connecting the grounding wire to the grounding rod serves a crucial function: it directly prevents electrical shock. This prevention is achieved by providing a low-resistance path for fault current to travel safely into the earth, thereby minimizing the risk of electrical shock to individuals who might come into contact with the system during a fault condition. This example vividly illustrates the clear and direct link between the specific action taken—properly connecting the grounding wire—and the resulting safety outcome, which is the mitigation of electrical shock hazards.

To effectively analyze these cause-and-effect relationships, it is essential to pay close attention to the verbs and connectors that explicitly indicate causality. Words and phrases such as "results in," "causes," "leads to," and "because" serve as critical indicators of these relationships. For instance, in the statement, "Exposing wires to moisture causes corrosion, leading to increased resistance and potential fire hazard," the terms "causes" and "leading to" are pivotal in highlighting the cause-and-effect chain. In this context, the exposure of wires to moisture initiates a chemical reaction that causes corrosion. This corrosion, in turn, increases the electrical resistance of the wires, which can lead to overheating and a subsequent fire hazard. Each step in this progression is causally linked, demonstrating how initial exposure to moisture sets off a chain of events that culminates in a significant safety risk.

Drawing Conclusions from Data

Aspiring electricians must possess a high degree of proficiency in synthesizing conclusions from diverse data types found within both technical documents and workplace-related texts, as this competency is crucial for excelling in the IBEW aptitude test and succeeding in their professional journeys. Mastery of this skill involves a meticulous examination of numerical datasets, detailed diagrams, and step-by-step procedural instructions to facilitate well-informed decision-making processes regarding electrical systems. For instance, when confronted with a schematic diagram illustrating an electrical circuit, it is imperative to accurately interpret the various symbols representing components such as resistors, capacitors, and power sources, comprehend the intricacies of their interconnections, and anticipate the circuit's operational behavior under varying conditions, such as changes in voltage or resistance.

Consider a schematic representation of a series circuit comprising a power source, a resistor, and a light bulb. The diagram specifies a power source of 12 volts, a resistor with a resistance of 8Ω, and a light bulb with a resistance of 4Ω. To derive meaningful conclusions from this setup, one must apply Ohm's Law, which articulates that the current (I) flowing through a circuit is the quotient of the voltage (V) across the circuit and the total resistance (R) within it. In this scenario, the total resistance is calculated as the sum of the individual resistances, $8\Omega + 4\Omega = 12\Omega$. Consequently, the current can be calculated using the formula $I = \dfrac{V}{R} = \dfrac{12V}{12\Omega} = 1A$.

This precise analysis indicates that the circuit will conduct a current of 1 Ampere.

Interpreting procedural data necessitates a comprehensive understanding of the sequential order and resultant effects of each procedural step. For example, a technical manual may specify that prior to conducting a test on a Ground Fault Circuit Interrupter (GFCI) outlet, it is essential to unplug all connected appliances from the circuit. This precautionary measure is crucial to prevent false readings or potential damage to the testing equipment. The instruction underscores a direct cause-and-effect relationship, where the act of unplugging appliances significantly influences the accuracy and safety of the testing procedure by eliminating extraneous variables that could skew results.

Effective data analysis also involves the ability to discern patterns and trends within datasets, such as fluctuations in electrical consumption over a specified time period. By plotting these data points on a graph, one can visually ascertain whether the electrical consumption is experiencing an upward trajectory, a downward trend, or remains relatively stable. This proficiency in graphical data interpretation is invaluable for diagnosing potential issues within electrical systems, such as inefficiencies or anomalies, and is instrumental in strategic planning for resource allocation and future system enhancements.

Acknowledgements

We extend our deepest gratitude to each individual committed to mastering the intricate skills required to successfully navigate the IBEW Aptitude Test. Your unwavering dedication to advancing within the electrical field is truly commendable, and we trust that this book has served as an indispensable resource in your preparation. Your investment of time and effort into understanding complex mathematical concepts, honing spatial reasoning abilities, and developing a firm grasp of mechanical comprehension reflects a profound commitment to your future career.

Your pursuit of both personal and professional development is the driving force behind the creation of this guide. Whether you are at the outset of your journey, contemplating a transition into the electrical field, or seeking to deepen your existing knowledge base, your chosen path is both respected and supported within these pages. The diverse array of experiences and backgrounds you bring to the electrical trade enriches the profession, infusing it with novel perspectives and unique strengths that contribute to its evolution.

Aspiring electricians, you are the essential framework of our contemporary society, ensuring that electrical systems function seamlessly, machinery operates efficiently, and residential environments remain secure and comfortable. The competencies you are cultivating in preparation for the IBEW Aptitude Test not only equip you for immediate success but also establish a robust foundation for a career that is consistently in high demand. Mastery of these skills ensures your ability to troubleshoot complex systems, implement innovative solutions, and contribute to the advancement of electrical technology.

Instructors and mentors, your profound impact on the development of aspiring electricians cannot be overstated. Through your dedication to imparting knowledge and providing guidance, you transform novices into adept professionals. This book is designed to augment the foundational knowledge you deliver, offering additional insights and strategies that align with your teaching. Your commitment to excellence fosters a culture of high standards and continuous improvement within the trade, reinforcing the quality and reliability of the workforce.

To all those who contribute to this collective endeavor, your relentless hard work, intellectual curiosity, and steadfast perseverance are the driving forces propelling the electrical industry forward. This book stands as a testament to the collective ambition and dedication of all involved, reflecting the shared goal of advancing the field through innovation and expertise.

HOW TO ACCESS THE BONUSES

SCAN THE QR CODE: